The LONDON and NORTH WESTERN RAILWAY

A Selection of 7mm Locomotive Drawings

Compiled by M. Sharman

The
OAKWOOD PRESS

Printed and Bound by
Bocardo Press, Cowley, Oxford

ISBN 0 85361 315 X

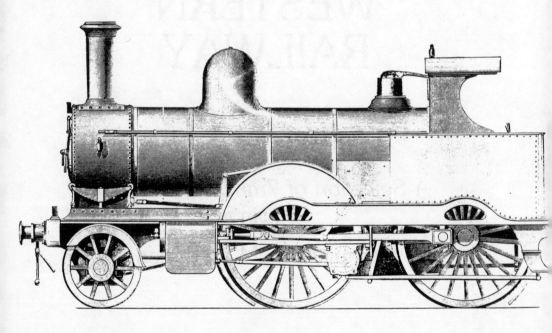

Published by
THE OAKWOOD PRESS
P.O. Box 122
Headington
Oxford

INTRODUCTION

This is the second volume in the Portfolio series, compiled to give the railway historian and enthusiast the opportunity to collect (in a worthwhile scale of 7mm to the foot), most of the varied and interesting drawings contained within the pages of *The Locomotive Magazine*. This has been made possible by the kind co-operation of the magazine's owners, Ian Allan Ltd, Coombelands, Surrey.

These drawings are complimentary to the many books that have been published over the years on the 'Premier line' i.e. the LNWR, and therefore can be studied in conjunction with them. To assist the reader therefore, I have listed a few of the allied publications below, but the LNWR has been so well documented, this bibliography covers only a very general selection.

Accompanying each drawing is found the date and page number as to when it appeared in *The Locomotive Magazine* and this will aid your research further, if you should wish to read the article.

The range of drawings depicted are not in anyway complete, in the sense that not all the LNWR classes are represented. This is mainly due to the fact that, as photography became established, the magazine discontinued the use of drawings in favour of the photograph.

There is a slight departure from the first volume as there was a shortage of tender drawings, the only drawings being available being the early Bury and Allan types. Therefore basic representation of the 1800 gallon and 3000 gallon tenders have been included but do beware of the differences, such as axle boxes, coal-rails, tool boxes, rivets etc, when used with various locomotive classes. Here make use of the reference works and study the relevant photographs of the actual class that interests you.

Further volumes in the series are listed on the back cover and are grouped by Railway Companies or regions etc, where possible. It is proposed to include foreign railways in the series as so many of these locomotives were designed and constructed by British manufacturers, such as Sharp Stewart, Stephensons, Neilsons, Vulcan, Dubbs etc.

I hope you find this second volume as exciting as volume one and I look forward to presenting to you more drawings in future volumes.

M. Sharman 1986

BIBLIOGRAPHY

The Locomotive Magazine
The Engineer
The Railway Magazine
The Railway Engineer
HMRS Journals
The British Steam Locomotives 1825–1925 – Ahrons
The Premier Line – O.S. Nock
Evolution of the Steam Railway
LNWR Miscellany Volume One and Two – E. Talbot
An Illustrated History of LNWR Engines – E. Talbot.

CONTENTS

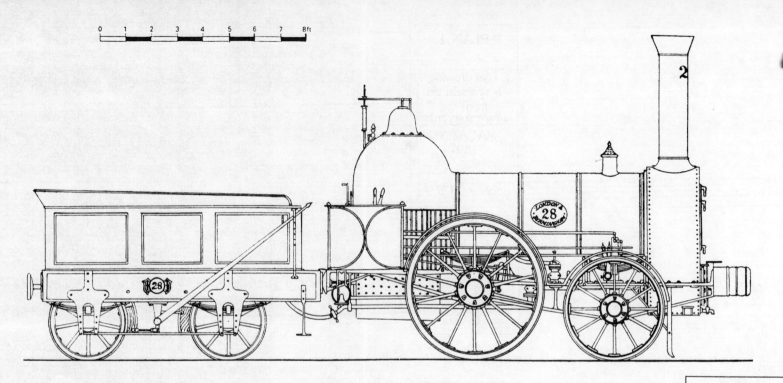

0 1 2 3 4 5 6 7 8ft

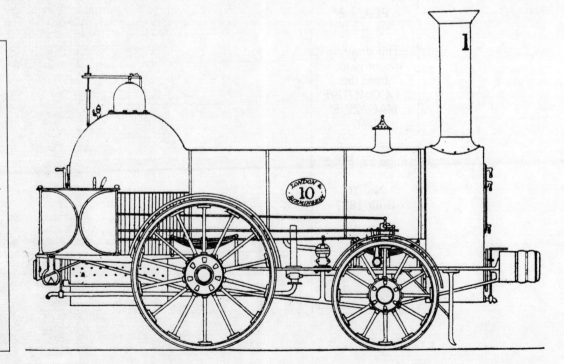

PLAN 1

*

This drawing
is reproduced
from the
LOCOMOTIVE
MAGAZINE
1897

Page 57, Fig. 1

**No. 28
Built 1837**

Rothwell
& Co

PLAN 2

*

This drawing
is reproduced
from the
LOCOMOTIVE
MAGAZINE
1897

Page 57, Fig. 2

**No. 10
Built 1837**

Hicks & Co.

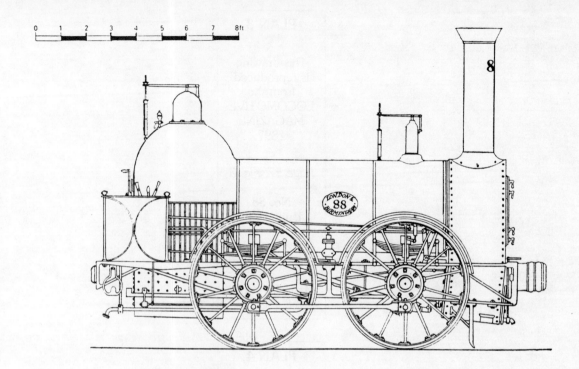

PLAN 3

*

This drawing
is reproduced
from the
LOCOMOTIVE
MAGAZINE
1897

Page 57, Fig. 3

**No. 88
Built 1839**

Maunslay, Sons
& Field

0 1 2 3 4 5 6 7 8ft

8

88

7

70

PLAN 4

*

This drawing
is reproduced
from the
LOCOMOTIVE
MAGAZINE
1897

Page 58, Fig. 4

**No. 70
Built 1839**

Bury & Co.

PLAN 3

*

This drawing
is reproduced
from the
LOCOMOTIVE
MAGAZINE
1897

Page 57, Fig. 3

No. 88
Built 1839

Maunslay, Sons
& Field

PLAN 4

*

This drawing
is reproduced
from the
LOCOMOTIVE
MAGAZINE
1897

Page 58, Fig. 4

No. 70
Built 1839

Bury & Co.

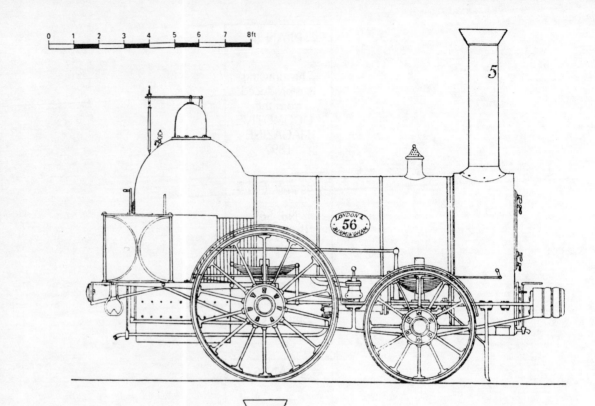

PLAN 5

*

This drawing
is reproduced
from the
LOCOMOTIVE
MAGAZINE
1897

Page 58, Fig. 5

**No. 56
Built 1841**

Bury & Co.

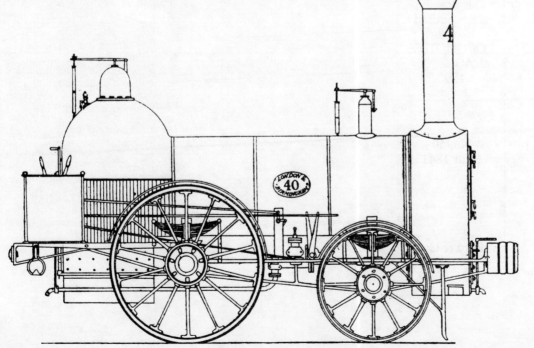

PLAN 6

*

This drawing
is reproduced
from the
LOCOMOTIVE
MAGAZINE
1897

Page 58, Fig. 6

**No. 40
Built 1841**

Bury & Co.

PLAN 5

*

This drawing
is reproduced
from the
LOCOMOTIVE
MAGAZINE
1897

Page 58, Fig. 5

**No. 56
Built 1841**

Bury & Co.

PLAN 6

*

This drawing
is reproduced
from the
LOCOMOTIVE
MAGAZINE
1897

Page 58, Fig. 6

**No. 40
Built 1841**

Bury & Co.

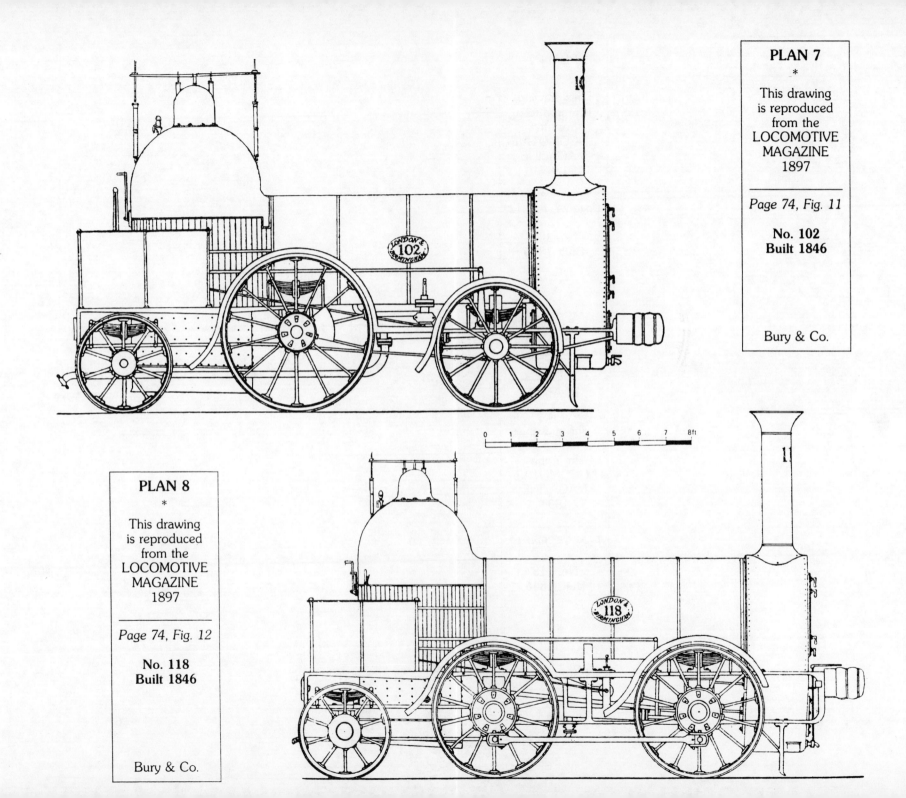

PLAN 7

*

This drawing
is reproduced
from the
LOCOMOTIVE
MAGAZINE
1897

Page 74, Fig. 11

**No. 102
Built 1846**

Bury & Co.

PLAN 8

*

This drawing
is reproduced
from the
LOCOMOTIVE
MAGAZINE
1897

Page 74, Fig. 12

**No. 118
Built 1846**

Bury & Co.

0 1 2 3 4 5 6 7 8ft

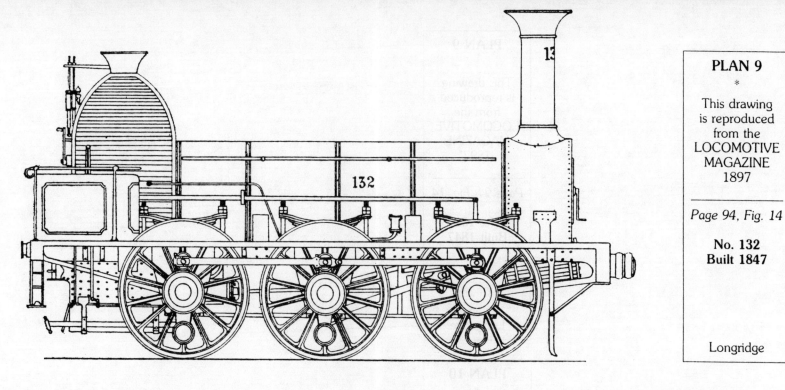

132

13

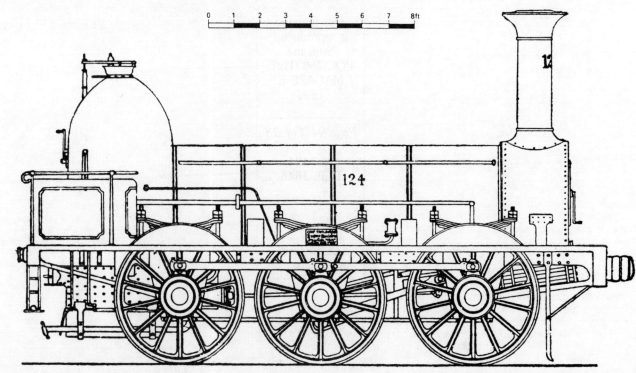

124

12

PLAN 9

*

This drawing
is reproduced
from the
LOCOMOTIVE
MAGAZINE
1897

Page 94, Fig. 14

**No. 132
Built 1847**

Longridge

PLAN 10

*

This drawing
is reproduced
from the
LOCOMOTIVE
MAGAZINE
1897

Page 94, Fig. 13

**No. 124
Built 1846**

C. Tayleur
& Co.

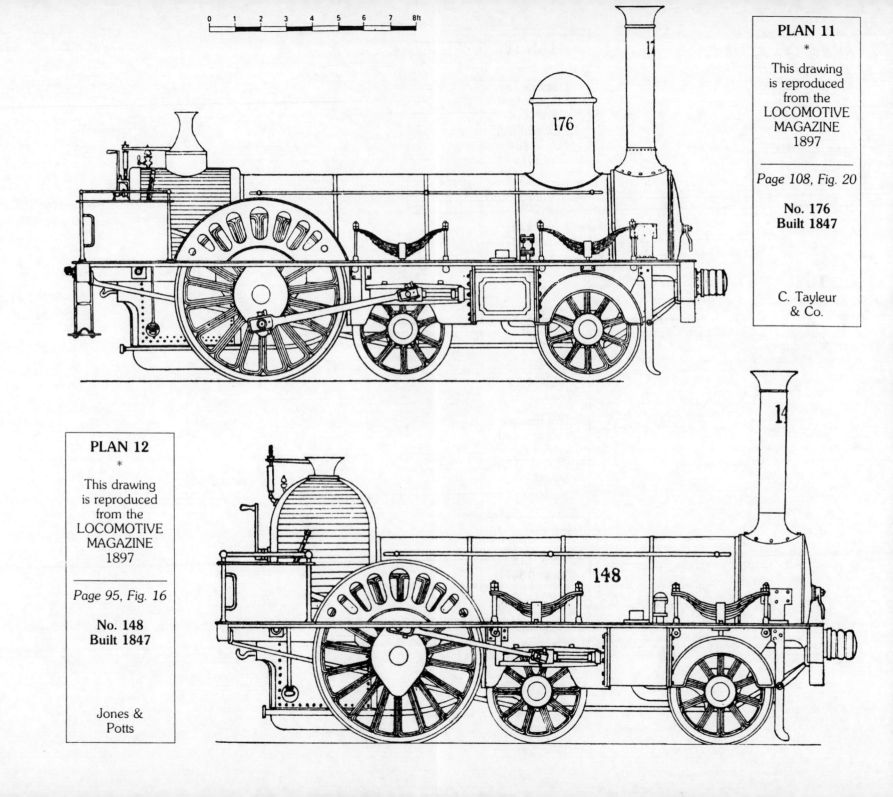

PLAN 11

*

This drawing
is reproduced
from the
LOCOMOTIVE
MAGAZINE
1897

Page 108, Fig. 20

**No. 176
Built 1847**

C. Tayleur
& Co.

176

17

PLAN 12

*

This drawing
is reproduced
from the
LOCOMOTIVE
MAGAZINE
1897

Page 95, Fig. 16

**No. 148
Built 1847**

Jones &
Potts

148

14

0 1 2 3 4 5 6 7 8ft

PLAN 11

*

This drawing
is reproduced
from the
LOCOMOTIVE
MAGAZINE
1897

Page 108, Fig. 20

**No. 176
Built 1847**

C. Tayleur
& Co.

PLAN 12

*

This drawing
is reproduced
from the
LOCOMOTIVE
MAGAZINE
1897

Page 95, Fig. 16

**No. 148
Built 1847**

Jones &
Potts

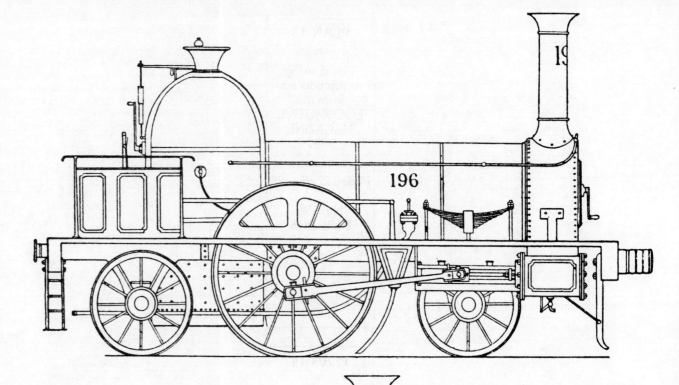

PLAN 13

*

This drawing
is reproduced
from the
LOCOMOTIVE
MAGAZINE
1897

Page 127, Fig. 23

**No. 196
Built 1848**

Nasmyth
& Co.

0 1 2 3 4 5 6 7 8ft

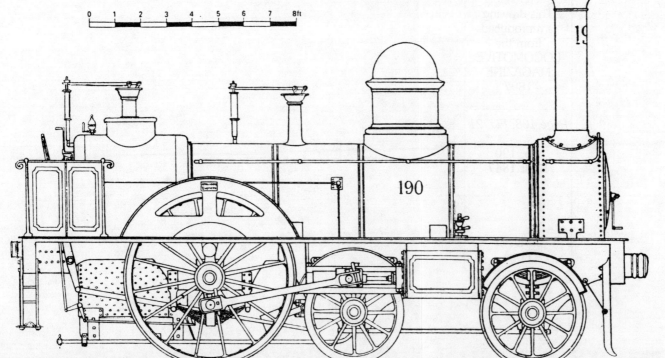

PLAN 14

*

This drawing
is reproduced
from the
LOCOMOTIVE
MAGAZINE
1897

Page 108, Fig. 21

**No. 190
Built 1847**

Jones &
Potts

PLAN 13

*

This drawing
is reproduced
from the
LOCOMOTIVE
MAGAZINE
1897

Page 127, Fig. 23

**No. 196
Built 1848**

Nasmyth
& Co.

PLAN 14

*

This drawing
is reproduced
from the
LOCOMOTIVE
MAGAZINE
1897

Page 108, Fig. 21

**No. 190
Built 1847**

Jones &
Potts

PLAN 15

*

This drawing
is reproduced
from the
LOCOMOTIVE
MAGAZINE
1897

Page 107, Fig. 17

No. 153
Built 1846

R. Stephenson
& Co.

0 1 2 3 4 5 6 7 8ft

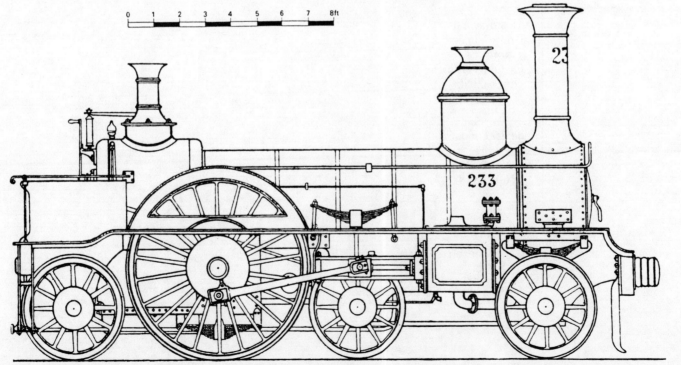

PLAN 16

*

This drawing
is reproduced
from the
LOCOMOTIVE
MAGAZINE
1897

Page 160, Fig. 35

No. 233
Built 1848

R. Stephenson
& Co.

PLAN 15

*

This drawing
is reproduced
from the
LOCOMOTIVE
MAGAZINE
1897

Page 107, Fig. 17

**No. 153
Built 1846**

R. Stephenson
& Co.

PLAN 16

*

This drawing
is reproduced
from the
LOCOMOTIVE
MAGAZINE
1897

Page 160, Fig. 35

**No. 233
Built 1848**

R. Stephenson
& Co.

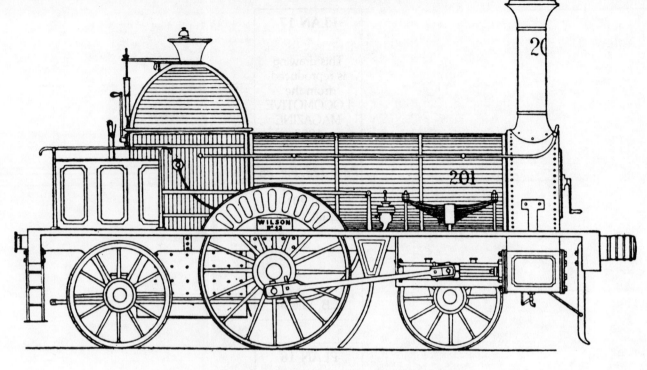

201

0 1 2 3 4 5 6 7 8ft

208

PLAN 17

*

This drawing
is reproduced
from the
LOCOMOTIVE
MAGAZINE
1897

_____

Page 128, Fig. 25

**No. 201
Built 1848**

E.B. Wilson

PLAN 18

*

This drawing
is reproduced
from the
LOCOMOTIVE
MAGAZINE
1897

_____

Page 143, Fig. 27

**No. 208
Built 1845**

E.B. Wilson

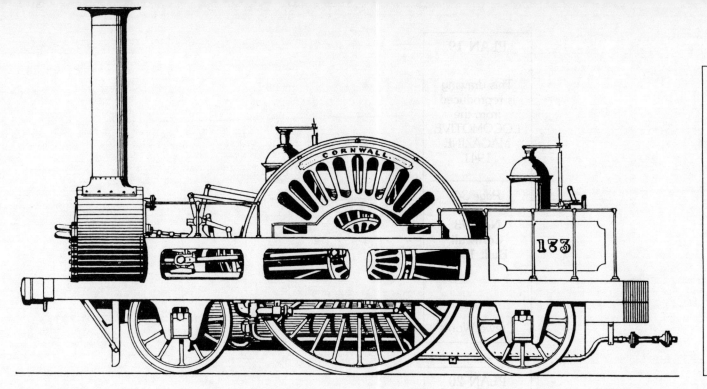

PLAN 19

*

This drawing
is reproduced
from the
LOCOMOTIVE
MAGAZINE
1941

Page 34

**No. 173
CORNWALL
Built 1847**

Crewe Works

PLAN 20

*

This drawing
is reproduced
from the
LOCOMOTIVE
MAGAZINE
1897

Page 174

**CORNWALL
Rebuilt 1847**

Crewe Works

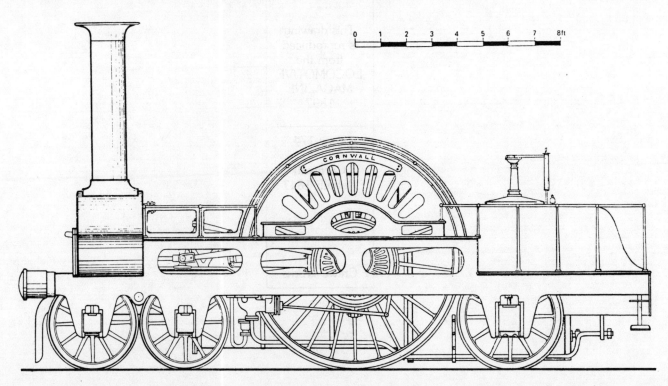

PLAN 19

*

This drawing
is reproduced
from the
LOCOMOTIVE
MAGAZINE
1941

Page 34

**No. 173
Cornwall
Built 1847**

Crewe Works

PLAN 20

*

This drawing
is reproduced
from the
LOCOMOTIVE
MAGAZINE
1897

Page 174

**Cornwall
Rebuilt 1847**

Crewe Works

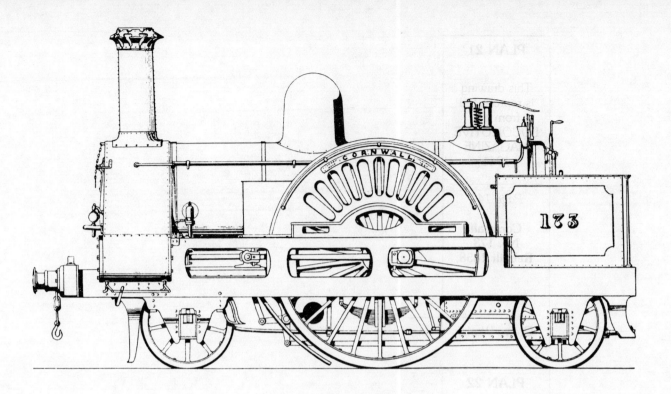

PLAN 21

*

This drawing
is reproduced
from the
LOCOMOTIVE
MAGAZINE
1941

Page 144

**CORNWALL
No. 173
Rebuilt 1858**

Crewe Works

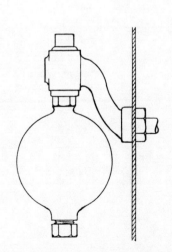

Ramsbottom's displacement lubricator
as fitted to "Cornwall."

PLAN 22

*

This drawing
is reproduced
from the
LOCOMOTIVE
MAGAZINE
1897

Page 128, Fig. 24

**LONDON
No. 200
Built 1847**

Tulk & Ley

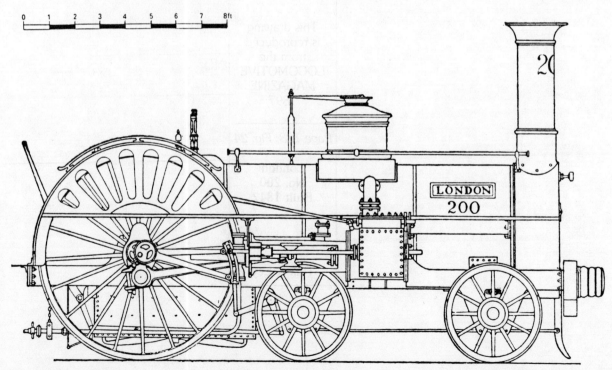

PLAN 21

*

This drawing
is reproduced
from the
LOCOMOTIVE
MAGAZINE
1941

Page 144

**Cornwall
No. 173
Rebuilt 1858**

Crewe Works

PLAN 22

*

This drawing
is reproduced
from the
LOCOMOTIVE
MAGAZINE
1897

Page 128, Fig. 24

**London
No. 200
Built 1847**

Tulk & Ley

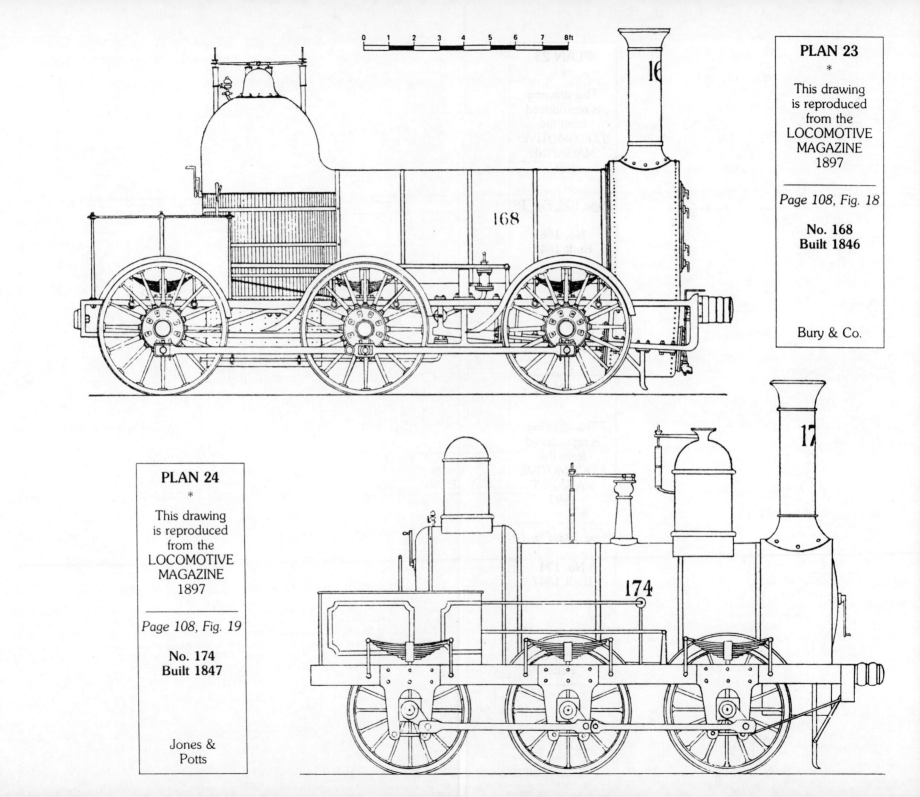

168

174

PLAN 23

*

This drawing
is reproduced
from the
LOCOMOTIVE
MAGAZINE
1897

―――――――

Page 108, Fig. 18

**No. 168
Built 1846**

Bury & Co.

PLAN 24

*

This drawing
is reproduced
from the
LOCOMOTIVE
MAGAZINE
1897

―――――――

Page 108, Fig. 19

**No. 174
Built 1847**

Jones &
Potts

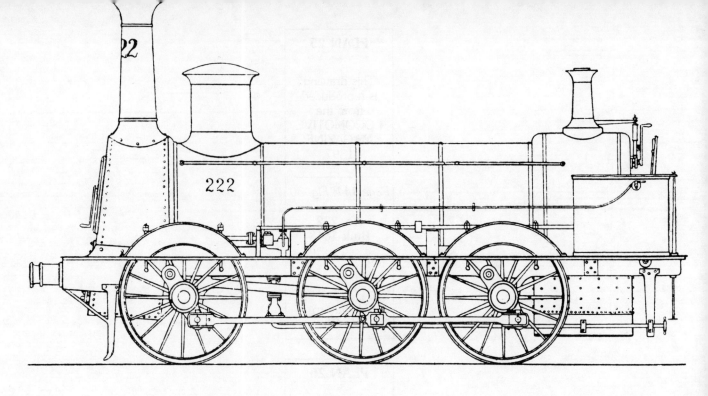

PLAN 25

*

This drawing
is reproduced
from the
LOCOMOTIVE
MAGAZINE
1897

Page 144, Fig. 30

**No. 222
Built 1848**

Hawthorn
& Co

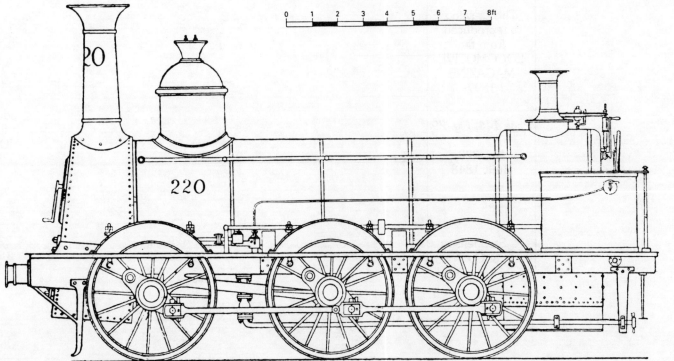

PLAN 26

*

This drawing
is reproduced
from the
LOCOMOTIVE
MAGAZINE
1897

Page 144, Fig. 29

**No. 220
Built 1848**

R. Stephenson
& Co.

PLAN 25

*

This drawing
is reproduced
from the
LOCOMOTIVE
MAGAZINE
1897

Page 144, Fig. 30

**No. 222
Built 1848**

Hawthorn
& Co

PLAN 26

*

This drawing
is reproduced
from the
LOCOMOTIVE
MAGAZINE
1897

Page 144, Fig. 29

**No. 220
Built 1848**

R. Stephenson
& Co.

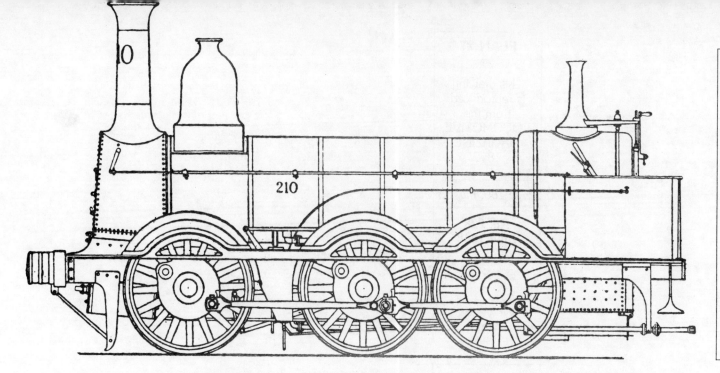

PLAN 27

*

This drawing
is reproduced
from the
LOCOMOTIVE
MAGAZINE
1897

Page 160, Fig. 33

**No. 228
Built 1848**

Wolverton
Works

PLAN 28

*

This drawing
is reproduced
from the
LOCOMOTIVE
MAGAZINE
1897

Page 144, Fig. 28

**No. 210
Built 1848**

Sharp Bros
& Co.

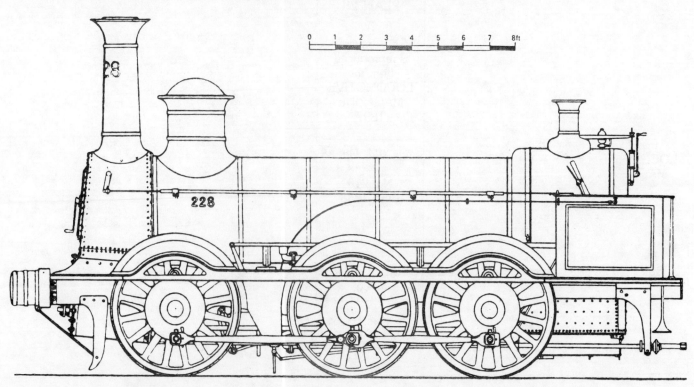

PLAN 27

*

This drawing
is reproduced
from the
LOCOMOTIVE
MAGAZINE
1897

Page 160, Fig. 33

**No. 228
Built 1848**

Wolverton
Works

PLAN 28

*

This drawing
is reproduced
from the
LOCOMOTIVE
MAGAZINE
1897

Page 144, Fig. 28

**No. 210
Built 1848**

Sharp Bros
& Co.

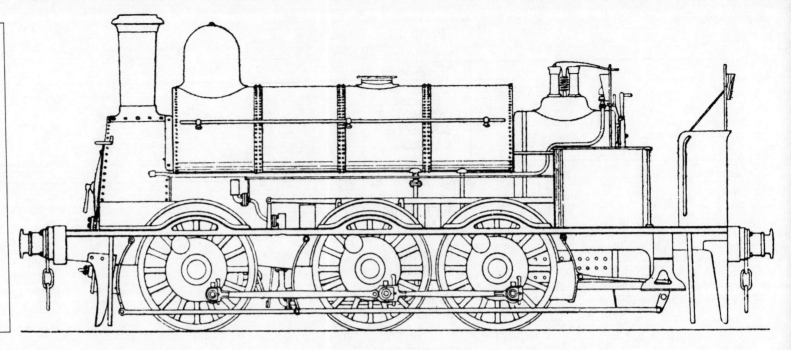

PLAN 29

*

This drawing
is reproduced
from the
LOCOMOTIVE
MAGAZINE
1905

Page 76, Fig. 10

**WREXHAM
MOLD
&
CONNAH'S
QUAY**

**Built 1854
Rebuilt 1873**

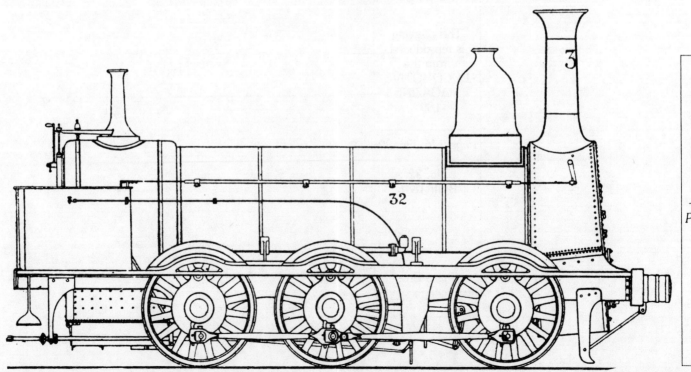

PLAN 30

*

This drawing
is reproduced
from the
LOCOMOTIVE
MAGAZINE
1897

Page 176, Fig. 39

**No. 32
Built 1846**

Sharp Bros

PLAN 29

*

This drawing
is reproduced
from the
LOCOMOTIVE
MAGAZINE
1905

Page 76, Fig. 10

**WREXHAM
MOLD
&
CONNAH'S
QUAY**

**Built 1854
Rebuilt 1873**

PLAN 30

*

This drawing
is reproduced
from the
LOCOMOTIVE
MAGAZINE
1897

Page 176, Fig. 39

**No. 32
Built 1846**

Sharp Bros

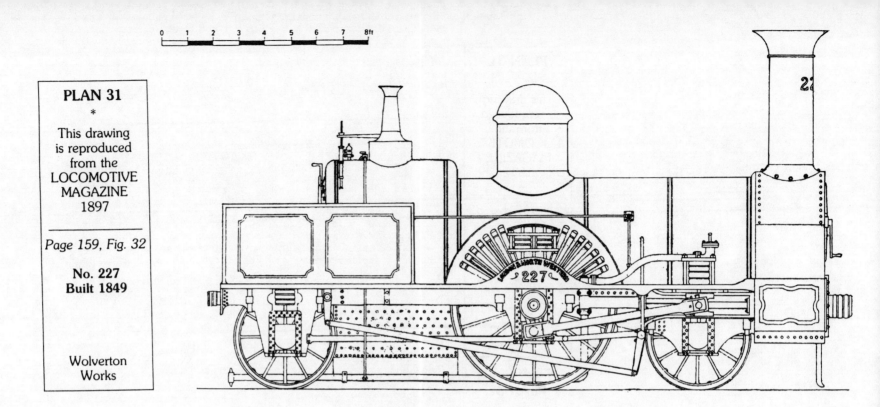

PLAN 31

*

This drawing
is reproduced
from the
LOCOMOTIVE
MAGAZINE
1897

Page 159, Fig. 32

**No. 227
Built 1849**

Wolverton
Works

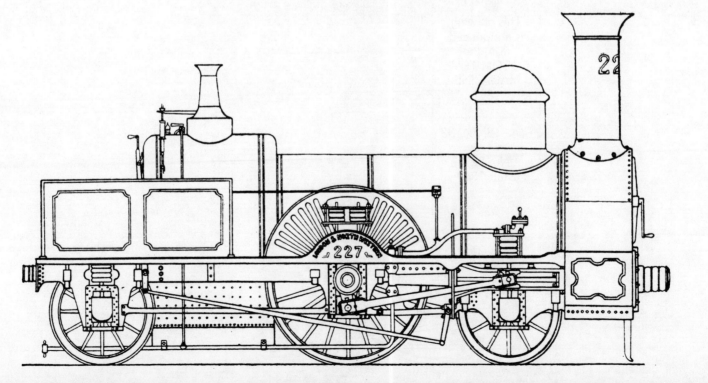

PLAN 32

*

This drawing
is reproduced
from the
LOCOMOTIVE
MAGAZINE
1897

Page 18, Fig. 32

**No. 227
Built 1849**

Wolverton
Works

PLAN 31

*

This drawing
is reproduced
from the
LOCOMOTIVE
MAGAZINE
1897

Page 159, Fig. 32

**No. 227
Built 1849**

Wolverton
Works

PLAN 32

*

This drawing
is reproduced
from the
LOCOMOTIVE
MAGAZINE
1897

Page 18, Fig. 32

**No. 227
Built 1849**

Wolverton
Works

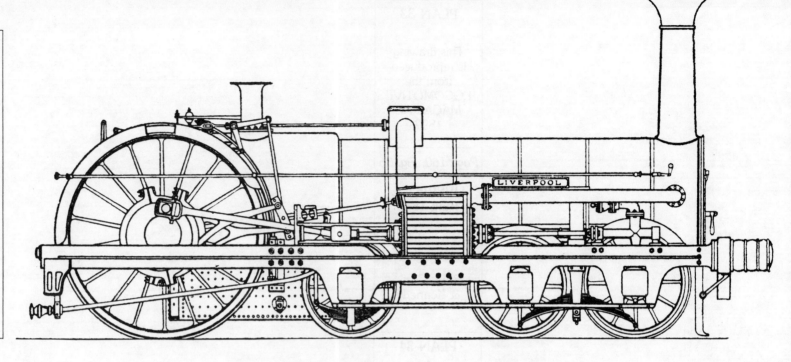

PLAN 33

*

This drawing
is reproduced
from the
LOCOMOTIVE
MAGAZINE
1897

Page 160, Fig. 36

**LIVERPOOL
Built 1848**

Bury, Curtis
& Kennedy

0 1 2 3 4 5 6 7 8ft

PLAN 34

*

This drawing
is reproduced
from the
LOCOMOTIVE
MAGAZINE
1941

Page 33

**COURIER
No. 176
Built 1847**

Crewe Works

PLAN 33

*

This drawing
is reproduced
from the
LOCOMOTIVE
MAGAZINE
1897

Page 160, Fig. 36

LIVERPOOL
Built 1848

Bury, Curtis
& Kennedy

PLAN 34

*

This drawing
is reproduced
from the
LOCOMOTIVE
MAGAZINE
1941

Page 33

COURIER
No. 176
Built 1847

Crewe Works

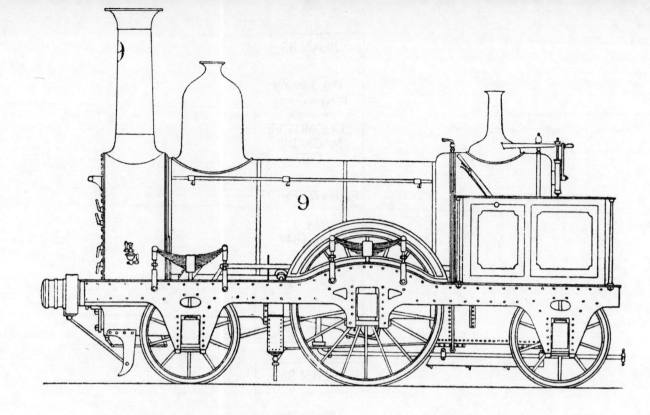

PLAN 35

*

This drawing
is reproduced
from the
LOCOMOTIVE
MAGAZINE
1897

Page 175, Fig. 37

**No. 9
Built 1847**

Sharp Bros

9

0 1 2 3 4 5 6 7 8ft

4

4

PLAN 36

*

This drawing
is reproduced
from the
LOCOMOTIVE
MAGAZINE
1897

Page 176, Fig. 38

**No. 4
Built 1847**

Sharp Bros

PLAN 35

*

This drawing
is reproduced
from the
LOCOMOTIVE
MAGAZINE
1897

———————

Page 175, Fig. 37

**No. 9
Built 1847**

Sharp Bros

PLAN 36

*

This drawing
is reproduced
from the
LOCOMOTIVE
MAGAZINE
1897

———————

Page 176, Fig. 38

**No. 4
Built 1847**

Sharp Bros

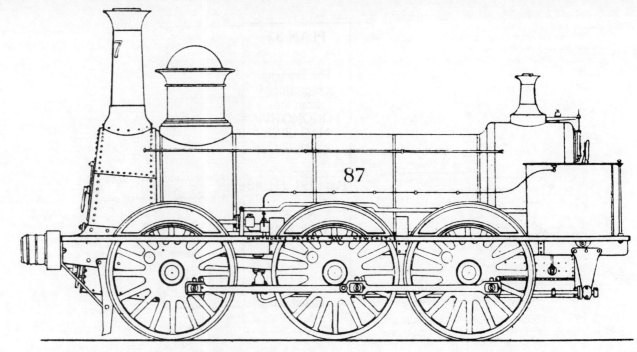

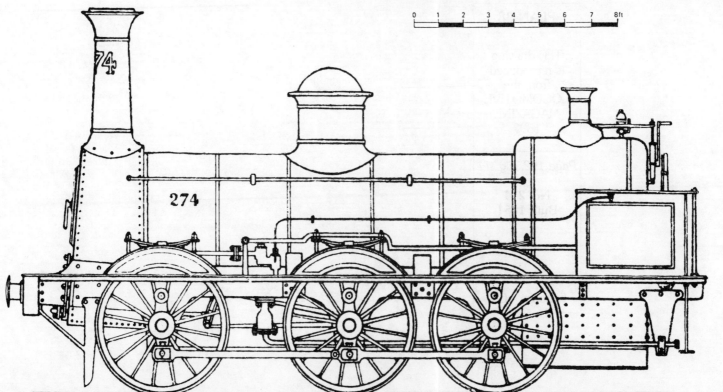

PLAN 37

*

This drawing
is reproduced
from the
LOCOMOTIVE
MAGAZINE
1897

Page 191, Fig. 42

**No. 87
Built 1848**

Hawthorn
& Co.

PLAN 38

*

This drawing
is reproduced
from the
LOCOMOTIVE
MAGAZINE
1897

Page 192, Fig. 44

**No. 274
Built 1851**

Fairburn's Co.

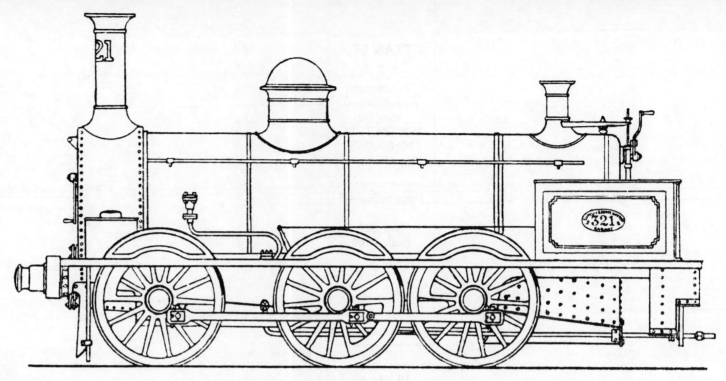

PLAN 39

*

This drawing
is reproduced
from the
LOCOMOTIVE
MAGAZINE
1898

Page 6, Fig. 48

**No. 321
Built 1854**

Kitson

0 1 2 3 4 5 6 7 8ft

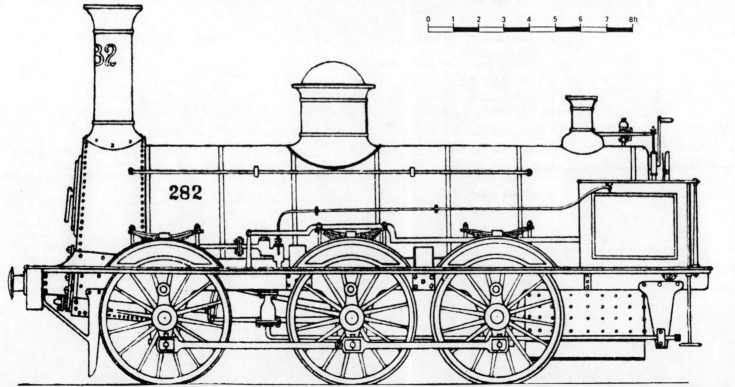

PLAN 40

*

This drawing
is reproduced
from the
LOCOMOTIVE
MAGAZINE
1897

Page 192, Fig. 48

**No. 282
Built 1854**

Fairburn's Co.

PLAN 39

*

This drawing
is reproduced
from the
LOCOMOTIVE
MAGAZINE
1898

Page 6, Fig. 48

**No. 321
Built 1854**

Kitson

PLAN 40

*

This drawing
is reproduced
from the
LOCOMOTIVE
MAGAZINE
1897

Page 192, Fig. 48

**No. 282
Built 1854**

Fairburn's Co.

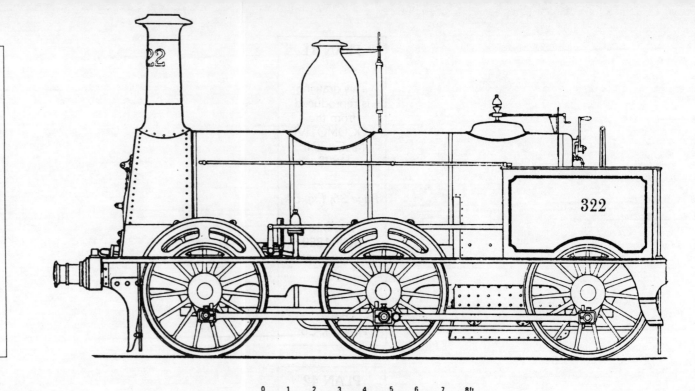

PLAN 41

*

This drawing
is reproduced
from the
LOCOMOTIVE
MAGAZINE
1898

Page 36, Fig. 54

**No. 322
Built 1859**

Beyer
Peacock Co.

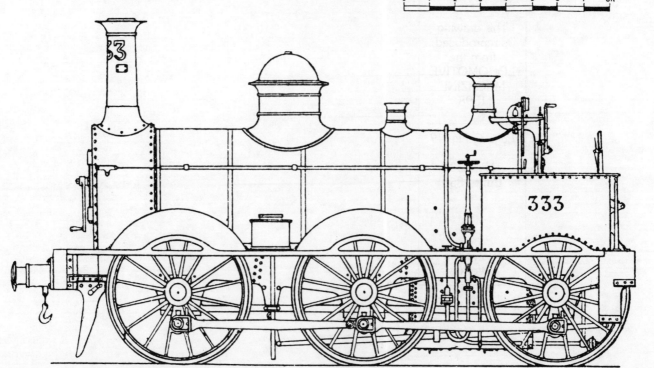

PLAN 42

*

This drawing
is reproduced
from the
LOCOMOTIVE
MAGAZINE
1898

Page 6, Fig. 49

**No. 333
Built 1856**

Wolverton
Works

PLAN 41

*

This drawing
is reproduced
from the
LOCOMOTIVE
MAGAZINE
1898

Page 36, Fig. 54

No. 322
Built 1859

Beyer
Peacock Co.

PLAN 42

*

This drawing
is reproduced
from the
LOCOMOTIVE
MAGAZINE
1898

Page 6, Fig. 49

No. 333
Built 1856

Wolverton
Works

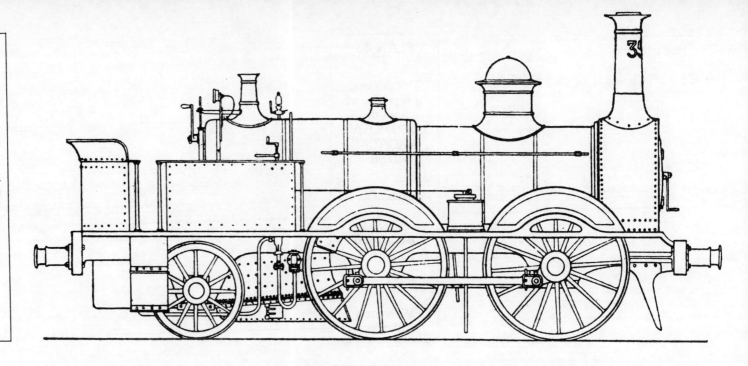

PLAN 43

*

This drawing
is reproduced
from the
LOCOMOTIVE
MAGAZINE
1898

Page 22, Fig. 53

**No. 354
Built 1860**

Wolverton
Works

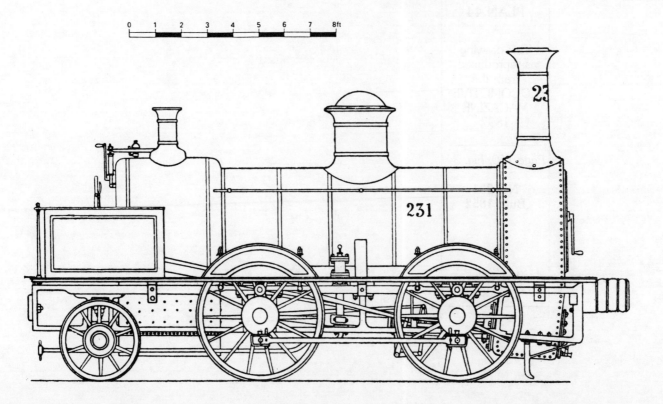

PLAN 44

*

This drawing
is reproduced
from the
LOCOMOTIVE
MAGAZINE
1897

Page 160, Fig. 34

**No. 231
Built 1852**

Wolverton
Works

0 1 2 3 4 5 6 7 8ft

PLAN 43

*

This drawing
is reproduced
from the
LOCOMOTIVE
MAGAZINE
1898

Page 22, Fig. 53

**No. 354
Built 1860**

Wolverton
Works

PLAN 44

*

This drawing
is reproduced
from the
LOCOMOTIVE
MAGAZINE
1897

Page 160, Fig. 34

**No. 231
Built 1852**

Wolverton
Works

PLAN 45

*

This drawing
is reproduced
from the
LOCOMOTIVE
MAGAZINE
1898

Page 54, Fig. 59

**No. 778
Built 1862**

Wolverton
Works

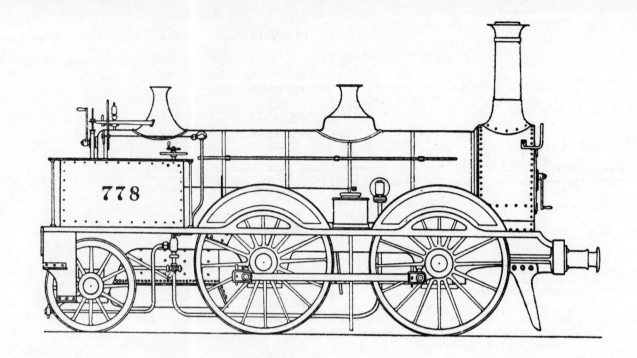

PLAN 46

*

This drawing
is reproduced
from the
LOCOMOTIVE
MAGAZINE
1898

Page 54, Fig. 60

**No. 734
Built 1862**

Wolverton
Works

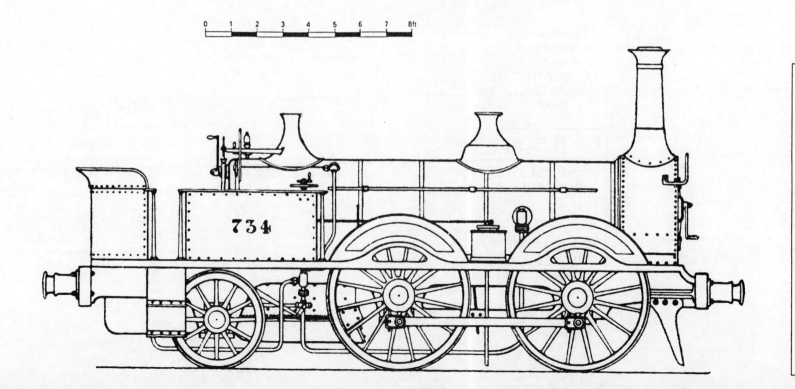

PLAN 45

*

This drawing
is reproduced
from the
LOCOMOTIVE
MAGAZINE
1898

Page 54, Fig. 59

**No. 778
Built 1862**

Wolverton
Works

PLAN 46

*

This drawing
is reproduced
from the
LOCOMOTIVE
MAGAZINE
1898

Page 54, Fig. 60

**No. 734
Built 1862**

Wolverton
Works

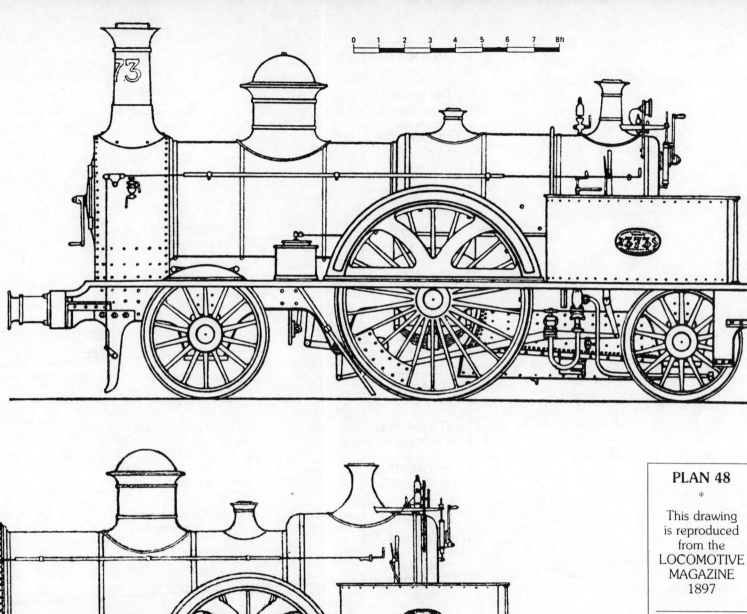

PLAN 47

*

This drawing
is reproduced
from the
LOCOMOTIVE
MAGAZINE
1898

Page 53, Fig. 58

**No. 373
Built 1861**

Wolverton
Works

PLAN 48

*

This drawing
is reproduced
from the
LOCOMOTIVE
MAGAZINE
1897

Page 191, Fig. 43

**No. 249
Built 1851**

Sharp Bros

0 1 2 3 4 5 6 7 8ft

PLAN 47

*

This drawing
is reproduced
from the
LOCOMOTIVE
MAGAZINE
1898

Page 53, Fig. 58

No. 373
Built 1861

Wolverton
Works

PLAN 48

*

This drawing
is reproduced
from the
LOCOMOTIVE
MAGAZINE
1897

Page 191, Fig. 43

No. 249
Built 1851

Sharp Bros

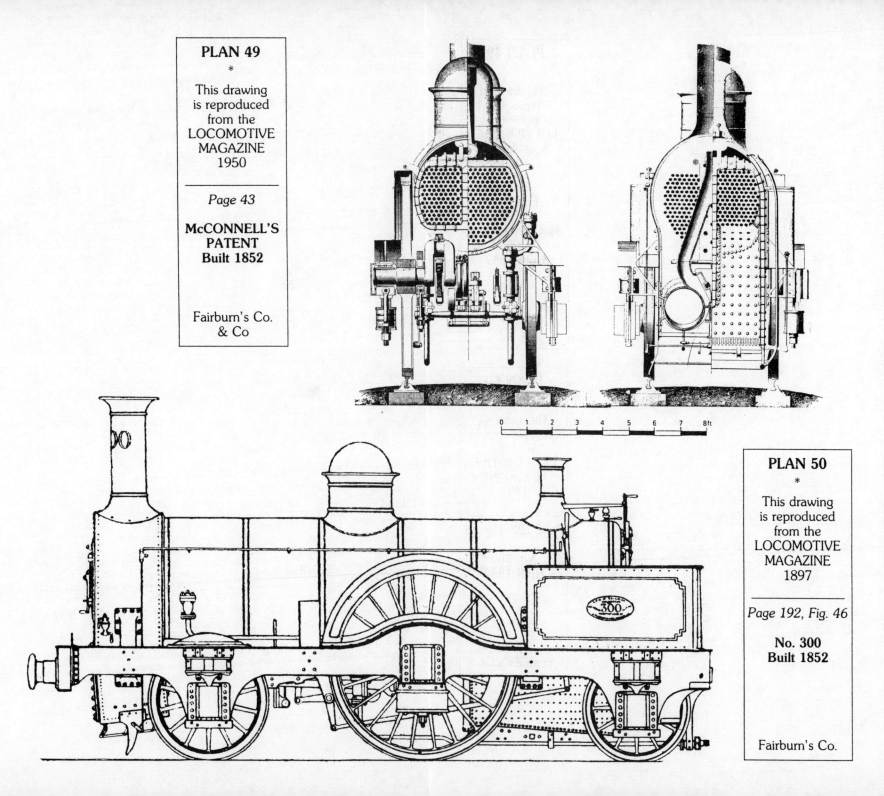

0 1 2 3 4 5 6 7 8ft

300

PLAN 49

*

This drawing
is reproduced
from the
LOCOMOTIVE
MAGAZINE
1950

Page 43

**McCONNELL'S
PATENT
Built 1852**

Fairburn's Co.
& Co

PLAN 50

*

This drawing
is reproduced
from the
LOCOMOTIVE
MAGAZINE
1897

Page 192, Fig. 46

**No. 300
Built 1852**

Fairburn's Co.

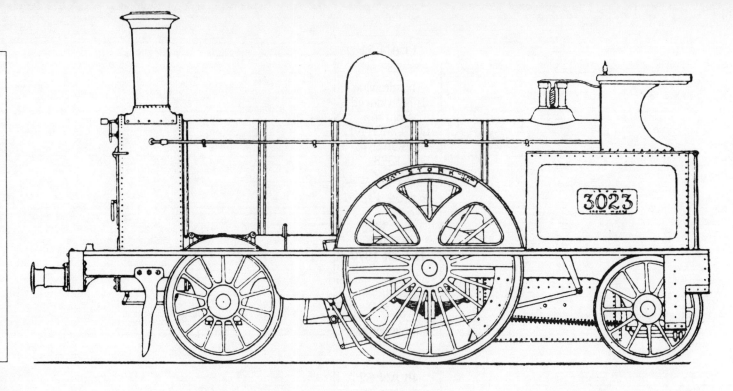

PLAN 51

*

This drawing
is reproduced
from the
LOCOMOTIVE
MAGAZINE
1898

Page 54, Fig. 61

**No. 3023
STORK
Rebuilt 1870**

Crewe Works

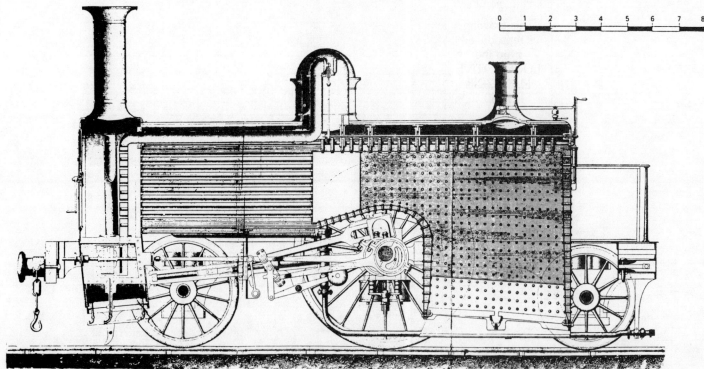

PLAN 52

*

This drawing
is reproduced
from the
LOCOMOTIVE
MAGAZINE
1950

Page 42

**McCONNELL'S
PATENT
(Section)
Built 1852**

Fairburn's Co.

0 1 2 3 4 5 6 7 8ft

PLAN 51

*

This drawing
is reproduced
from the
LOCOMOTIVE
MAGAZINE
1898

Page 54, Fig. 61

**No. 3023
STORK
Rebuilt 1870**

Crewe Works

PLAN 52

*

This drawing
is reproduced
from the
LOCOMOTIVE
MAGAZINE
1950

Page 42

**McCONNELL'S
PATENT
(Section)
Built 1852**

Fairburn's Co.

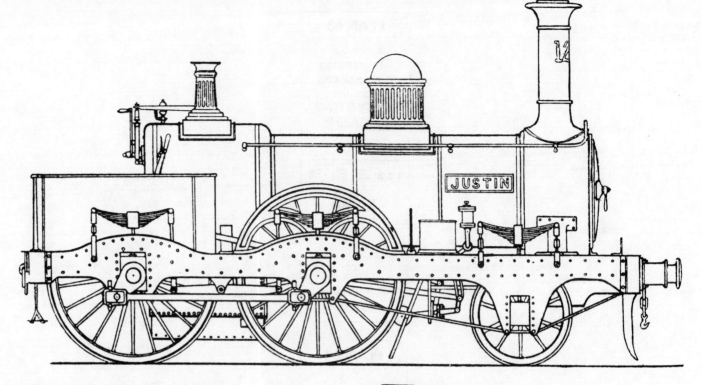

PLAN 53

*

This drawing
is reproduced
from the
LOCOMOTIVE
MAGAZINE
1898

Page 22, Fig. 52

JUSTIN
Built 1850

E.B. Wilson
& Co.

0 1 2 3 4 5 6 7 8ft

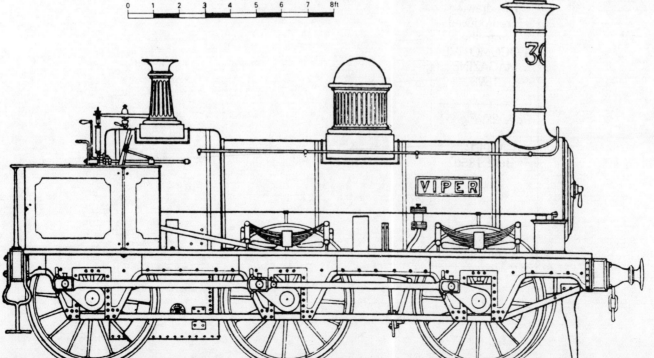

PLAN 54

*

This drawing
is reproduced
from the
LOCOMOTIVE
MAGAZINE
1898

Page 22, Fig. 51

VIPER
Built 1850

E.B. Wilson
& Co.

PLAN 53

*

This drawing
is reproduced
from the
LOCOMOTIVE
MAGAZINE
1898

Page 22, Fig. 52

JUSTIN
Built 1850

E.B. Wilson
& Co.

PLAN 54

*

This drawing
is reproduced
from the
LOCOMOTIVE
MAGAZINE
1898

Page 22, Fig. 51

VIPER
Built 1850

E.B. Wilson
& Co.

Comparative Sections of Ramsbottom's
and Webb's chimney caps.

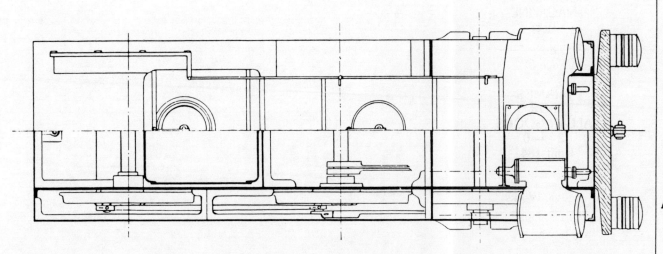

PLAN 55

*

This drawing
is reproduced
from the
LOCOMOTIVE
MAGAZINE
1941

Page 36

**No. 292
HARDWICKE
Built 1856**

Crewe Works

PLAN 56

*

This drawing
is reproduced
from the
LOCOMOTIVE
MAGAZINE
1941

Page 32

**FRAMES
FOR
ALLAN GOODS
2–4–0
Built 1841**

Crewe Works

PLAN 57

*

This drawing
is reproduced
from the
LOCOMOTIVE
MAGAZINE
1898

Page 37, Fig. 55

**No. 320
Built 1850**

Allan

PLAN 58

*

This drawing
is reproduced
from the
LOCOMOTIVE
MAGAZINE
1898

Page 37, Fig. 57

**No. 345
Built 1846**

Allan

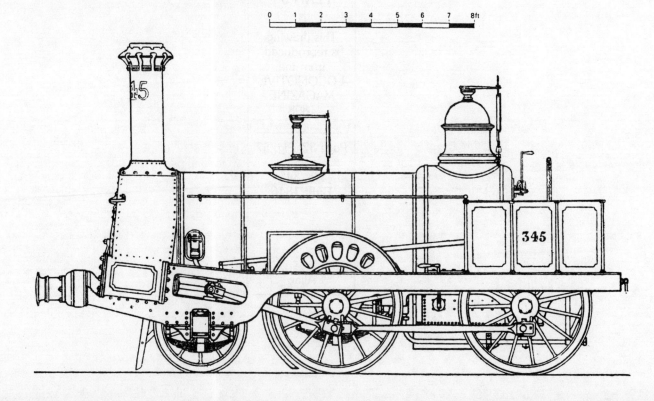

PLAN 57

*

This drawing
is reproduced
from the
LOCOMOTIVE
MAGAZINE
1898

Page 37, Fig. 55

**No. 320
Built 1850**

Allan

PLAN 58

*

This drawing
is reproduced
from the
LOCOMOTIVE
MAGAZINE
1898

Page 37, Fig. 57

**No. 345
Built 1846**

Allan

PLAN 59

*

This drawing
is reproduced
from the
LOCOMOTIVE
MAGAZINE
1943

Page 96

**VELOCIPEDE
Built 1847**

Allan

0 1 2 3 4 5 6 7 8ft

PLAN 60

*

This drawing
is reproduced
from the
LOCOMOTIVE
MAGAZINE
1941

Page 33

**VELOCIPEDE
No. 1932
Rebuilt 1869**

Crewe Works

PLAN 59

*

This drawing
is reproduced
from the
LOCOMOTIVE
MAGAZINE
1943

Page 96

**VELOCIPEDE
Built 1847**

Allan

PLAN 60

*

This drawing
is reproduced
from the
LOCOMOTIVE
MAGAZINE
1941

Page 33

**VELOCIPEDE
No. 1932
Rebuilt 1869**

Crewe Works

PLAN 61

*

This drawing
is reproduced
from the
LOCOMOTIVE
MAGAZINE
1942

Page 177

**No. 1874
COMPOUND
Rebuilt 1878**

Crewe Works

0 1 2 3 4 5 6 7 8ft

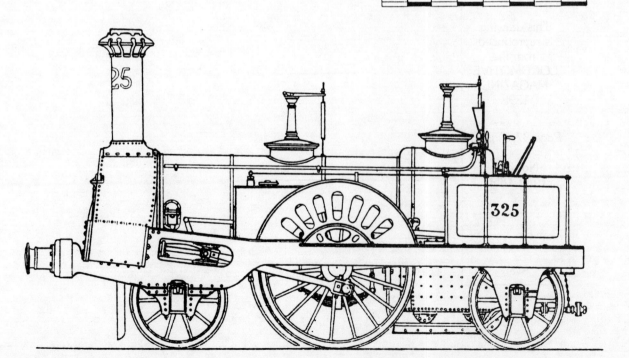

PLAN 62

*

This drawing
is reproduced
from the
LOCOMOTIVE
MAGAZINE
1898

Page 37, Fig. 56

**No. 325
Built 1850**

Allan

PLAN 61

*

This drawing
is reproduced
from the
LOCOMOTIVE
MAGAZINE
1942

Page 177

**No. 1874
COMPOUND
Rebuilt 1878**

Crewe Works

PLAN 62

*

This drawing
is reproduced
from the
LOCOMOTIVE
MAGAZINE
1898

Page 37, Fig. 56

**No. 325
Built 1850**

Allan

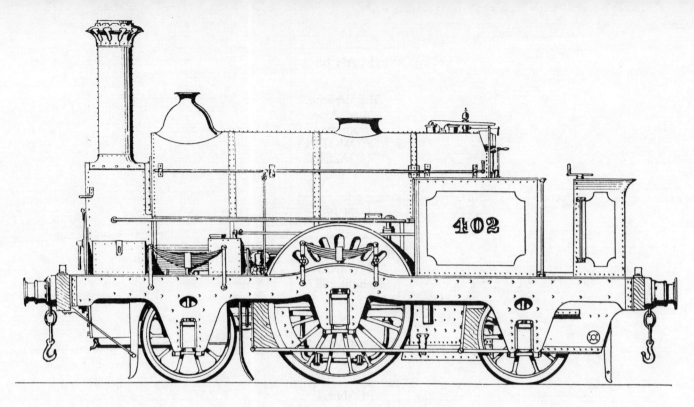

PLAN 63

*

This drawing
is reproduced
from the
LOCOMOTIVE
MAGAZINE
1941

Page 145

**No. 402
(FROM TENDER
ENGINE)**
Rebuilt 1857

Crewe Works

0 1 2 3 4 5 6 7 8ft

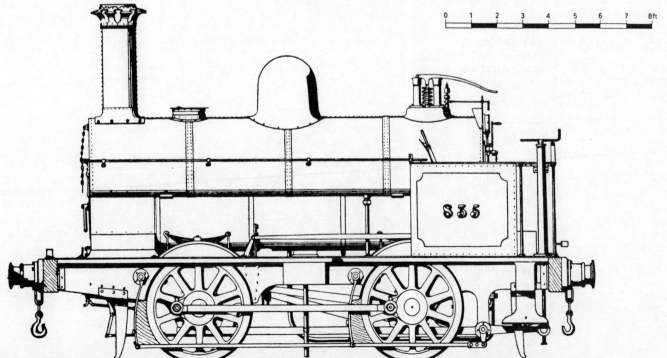

PLAN 64

*

This drawing
is reproduced
from the
LOCOMOTIVE
MAGAZINE
1941

Page 181

**No. 835
Built 1863**

Crewe Works

PLAN 63

*

This drawing
is reproduced
from the
LOCOMOTIVE
MAGAZINE
1941

Page 145

No. 402
(FROM TENDER
ENGINE)
Rebuilt 1857

Crewe Works

PLAN 64

*

This drawing
is reproduced
from the
LOCOMOTIVE
MAGAZINE
1941

Page 181

No. 835
Built 1863

Crewe Works

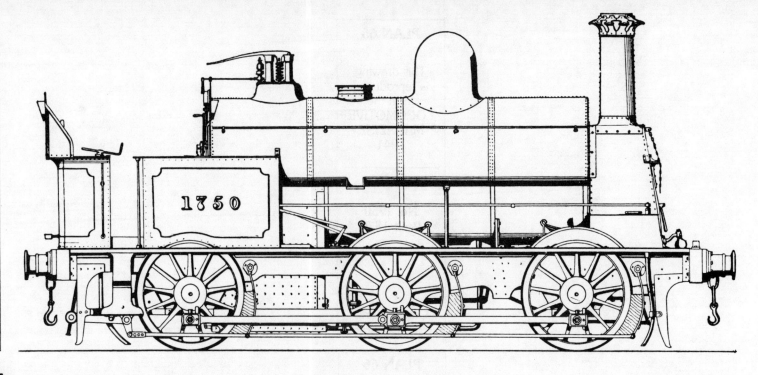

0 1 2 3 4 5 6 7 8ft

PLAN 65

*

This drawing
is reproduced
from the
LOCOMOTIVE
MAGAZINE
1941

Page 182

No. 1750
Built 1870

Crewe Works

PLAN 66

*

This drawing
is reproduced
from the
LOCOMOTIVE
MAGAZINE
1941

Page 145

No. 355
DX GOODS
HARDMAN
Built 1858

Crewe Works

PLAN 67

*

This drawing
is reproduced
from the
LOCOMOTIVE
MAGAZINE
1941

Page 181

No. 1480
NEWTON
Built 1863

Crewe Works

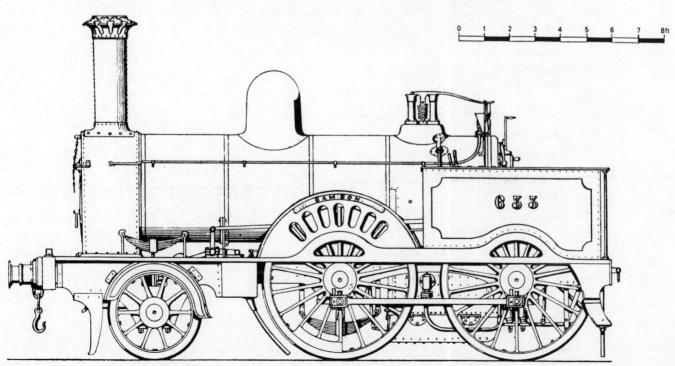

PLAN 68

*

This drawing
is reproduced
from the
LOCOMOTIVE
MAGAZINE
1941

Page 180

No. 633
SAMSON
Built 1863

Crewe Works

PLAN 67

*

This drawing
is reproduced
from the
LOCOMOTIVE
MAGAZINE
1941

Page 181

**No. 1480
NEWTON
Built 1863**

Crewe Works

PLAN 68

*

This drawing
is reproduced
from the
LOCOMOTIVE
MAGAZINE
1941

Page 180

**No. 633
SAMSON
Built 1863**

Crewe Works

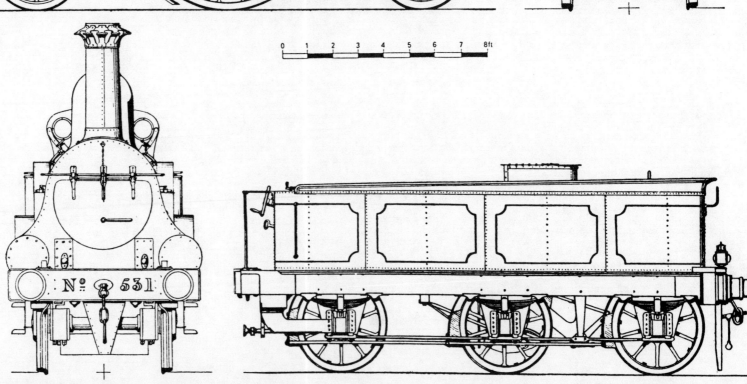

PLAN 69

*

This drawing
is reproduced
from the
LOCOMOTIVE
MAGAZINE
1941

Page 178

**No. 531
LADY OF
THE LAKE
Built 1859**

Crewe Works

0 1 2 3 4 5 6 7 8ft

PLAN 69

*

This drawing
is reproduced
from the
LOCOMOTIVE
MAGAZINE
1941

Page 178

**No. 531
LADY OF
THE LAKE
Built 1859**

Crewe Works

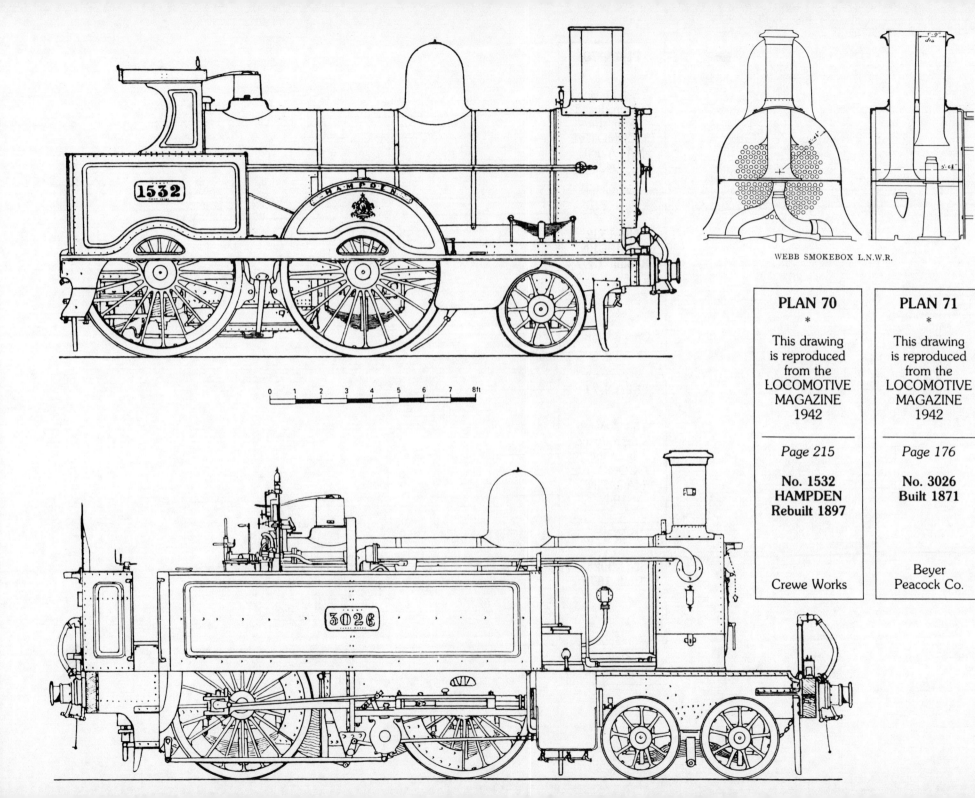

WEBB SMOKEBOX L.N.W.R.

PLAN 70	PLAN 71
*	*
This drawing is reproduced from the LOCOMOTIVE MAGAZINE 1942	This drawing is reproduced from the LOCOMOTIVE MAGAZINE 1942
Page 215	Page 176
No. 1532 HAMPDEN Rebuilt 1897	No. 3026 Built 1871
Crewe Works	Beyer Peacock Co.

PLAN 70

*

This drawing
is reproduced
from the
LOCOMOTIVE
MAGAZINE
1942

Page 215

**No. 1532
HAMPDEN
Rebuilt 1897**

Crewe Works

PLAN 71

*

This drawing
is reproduced
from the
LOCOMOTIVE
MAGAZINE
1942

Page 176

**No. 3026
Built 1871**

Beyer
Peacock Co.

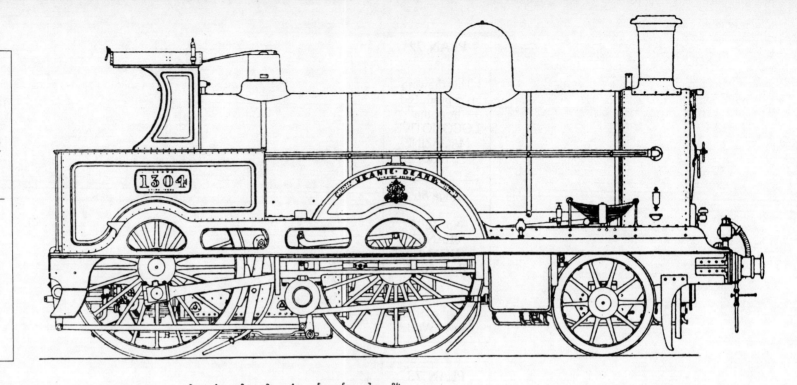

PLAN 72

*

This drawing
is reproduced
from the
LOCOMOTIVE
MAGAZINE
1938

Page 86

No. 1304
JEANIE
DEANE
Built 1888

Crewe Works

0 1 2 3 4 5 6 7 8ft

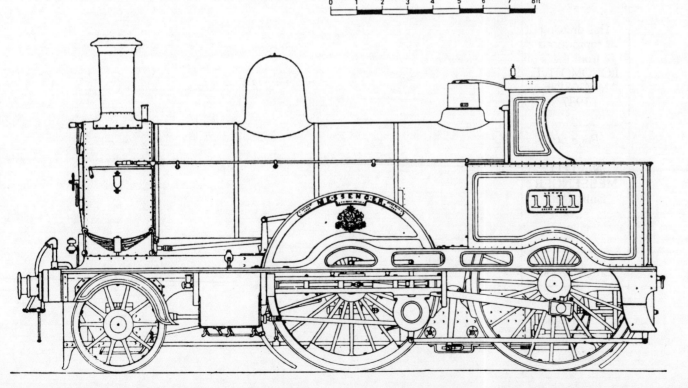

PLAN 73

*

This drawing
is reproduced
from the
LOCOMOTIVE
MAGAZINE
1937

Page 60

No. 1111
MESSENGER
Built 1882

Crewe Works

PLAN 72

*

This drawing
is reproduced
from the
LOCOMOTIVE
MAGAZINE
1938

Page 86

**No. 1304
JEANIE
DEANE
Built 1888**

Crewe Works

PLAN 73

*

This drawing
is reproduced
from the
LOCOMOTIVE
MAGAZINE
1937

Page 60

**No. 1111
MESSENGER
Built 1882**

Crewe Works

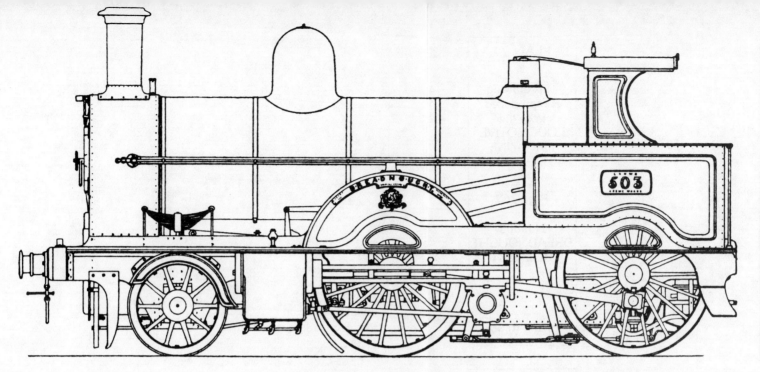

PLAN 74

*

This drawing
is reproduced
from the
LOCOMOTIVE
MAGAZINE
1937

Page 163

No. 503
DREADNOUGHT
Built 1884

Crewe Works

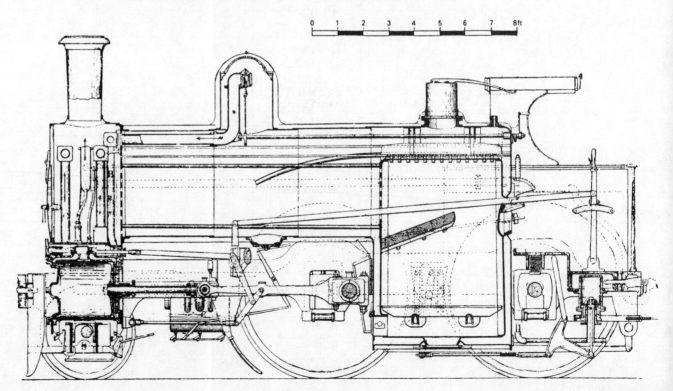

PLAN 75

*

This drawing
is reproduced
from the
LOCOMOTIVE
MAGAZINE
1937

SECTION
OF
No. 1111
Built 1882

Crewe Works

PLAN 74

*

This drawing
is reproduced
from the
LOCOMOTIVE
MAGAZINE
1937

Page 163

No. 503
DREADNOUGHT
Built 1884

Crewe Works

PLAN 75

*

This drawing
is reproduced
from the
LOCOMOTIVE
MAGAZINE
1937

SECTION
OF
No. 1111
Built 1882

Crewe Works

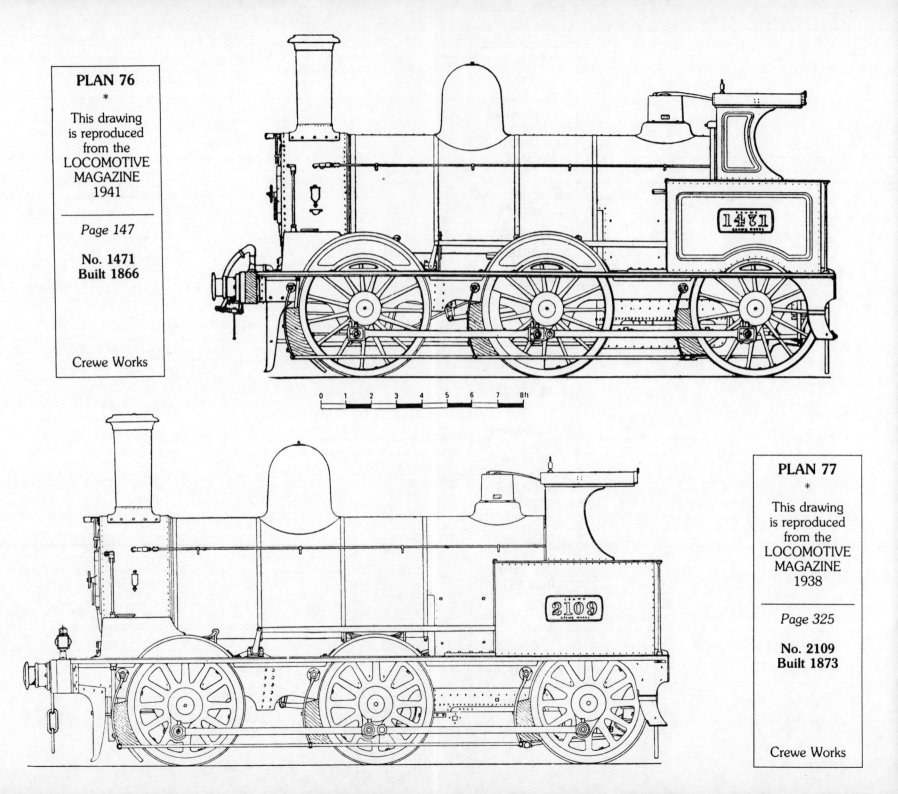

PLAN 76

*

This drawing
is reproduced
from the
LOCOMOTIVE
MAGAZINE
1941

Page 147

**No. 1471
Built 1866**

Crewe Works

0 1 2 3 4 5 6 7 8ft

PLAN 77

*

This drawing
is reproduced
from the
LOCOMOTIVE
MAGAZINE
1938

Page 325

**No. 2109
Built 1873**

Crewe Works

PLAN 76

*

This drawing
is reproduced
from the
LOCOMOTIVE
MAGAZINE
1941

Page 147

No. 1471
Built 1866

Crewe Works

PLAN 77

*

This drawing
is reproduced
from the
LOCOMOTIVE
MAGAZINE
1938

Page 325

No. 2109
Built 1873

Crewe Works

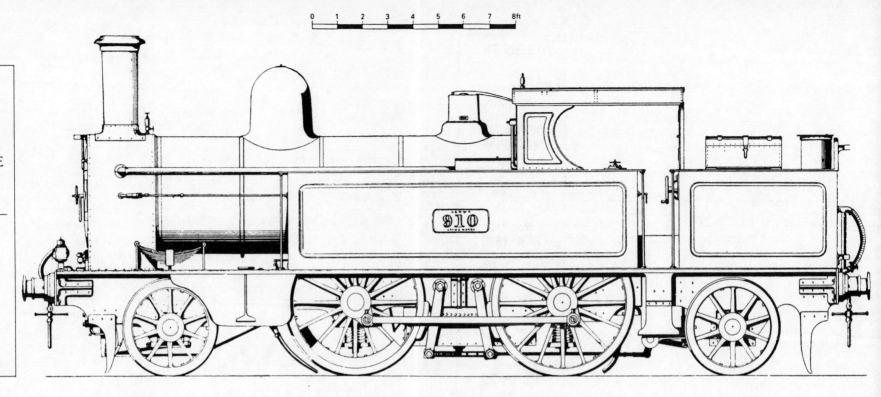

PLAN 78

*

This drawing
is reproduced
from the
LOCOMOTIVE
MAGAZINE
1842

Page 177

**No. 910
Built 1890**

Crewe Works

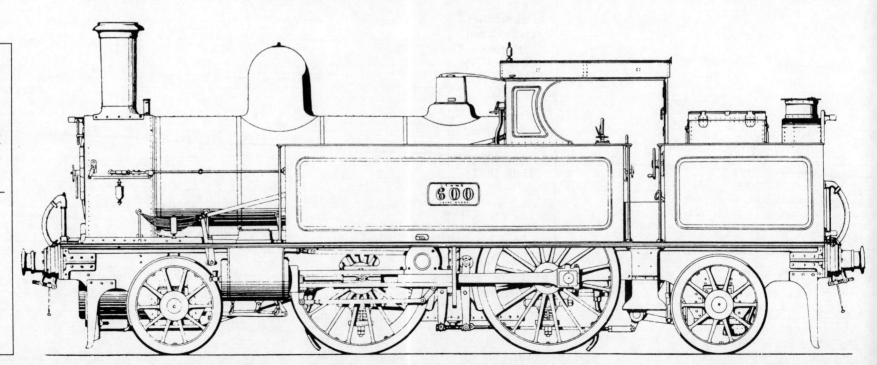

PLAN 79

*

This drawing
is reproduced
from the
LOCOMOTIVE
MAGAZINE
1942

Page 176

**No. 600
Built 1887**

Crewe Works

PLAN 78

*

This drawing
is reproduced
from the
LOCOMOTIVE
MAGAZINE
1842

Page 177

**No. 910
Built 1890**

Crewe Works

PLAN 79

*

This drawing
is reproduced
from the
LOCOMOTIVE
MAGAZINE
1942

Page 176

**No. 600
Built 1887**

Crewe Works

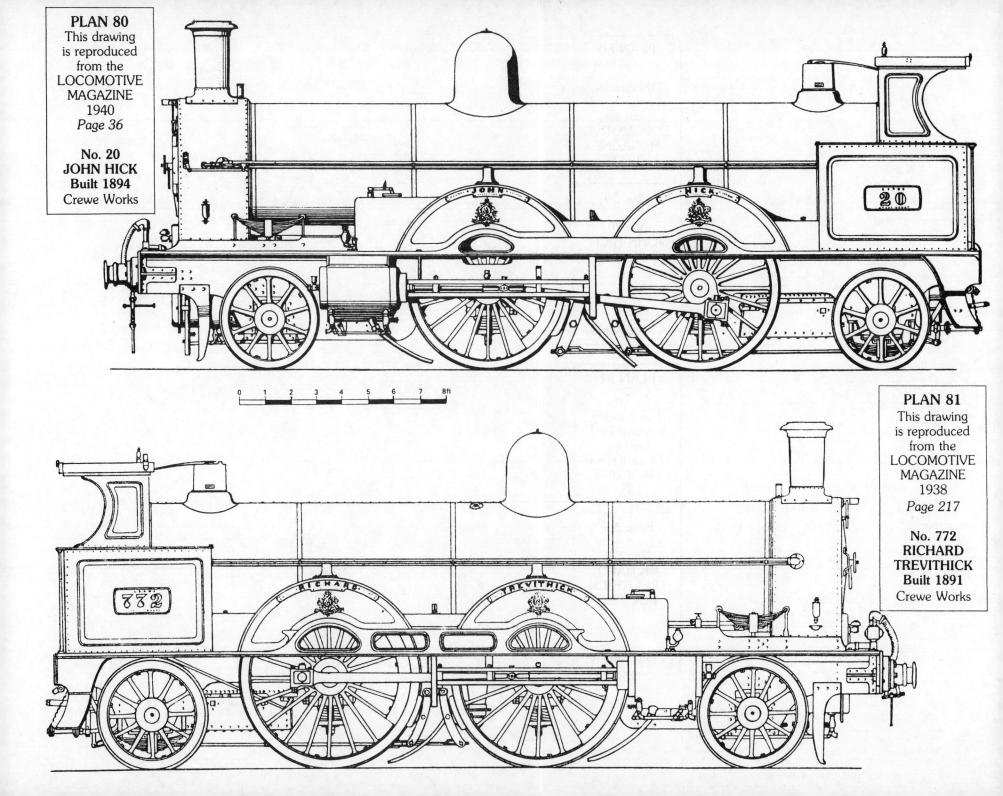

PLAN 80
This drawing
is reproduced
from the
LOCOMOTIVE
MAGAZINE
1940
Page 36

No. 20
JOHN HICK
Built 1894
Crewe Works

PLAN 81
This drawing
is reproduced
from the
LOCOMOTIVE
MAGAZINE
1938
Page 217

No. 772
RICHARD
TREVITHICK
Built 1891
Crewe Works

0 1 2 3 4 5 6 7 8ft

PLAN 80

*

This drawing
is reproduced
from the
LOCOMOTIVE
MAGAZINE
1940

Page 36

**No. 20
JOHN HICK
Built 1894**

Crewe Works

PLAN 81

*

This drawing
is reproduced
from the
LOCOMOTIVE
MAGAZINE
1938

Page 217

**No. 772
RICHARD
TREVITHICK
Built 1891**

Crewe Works

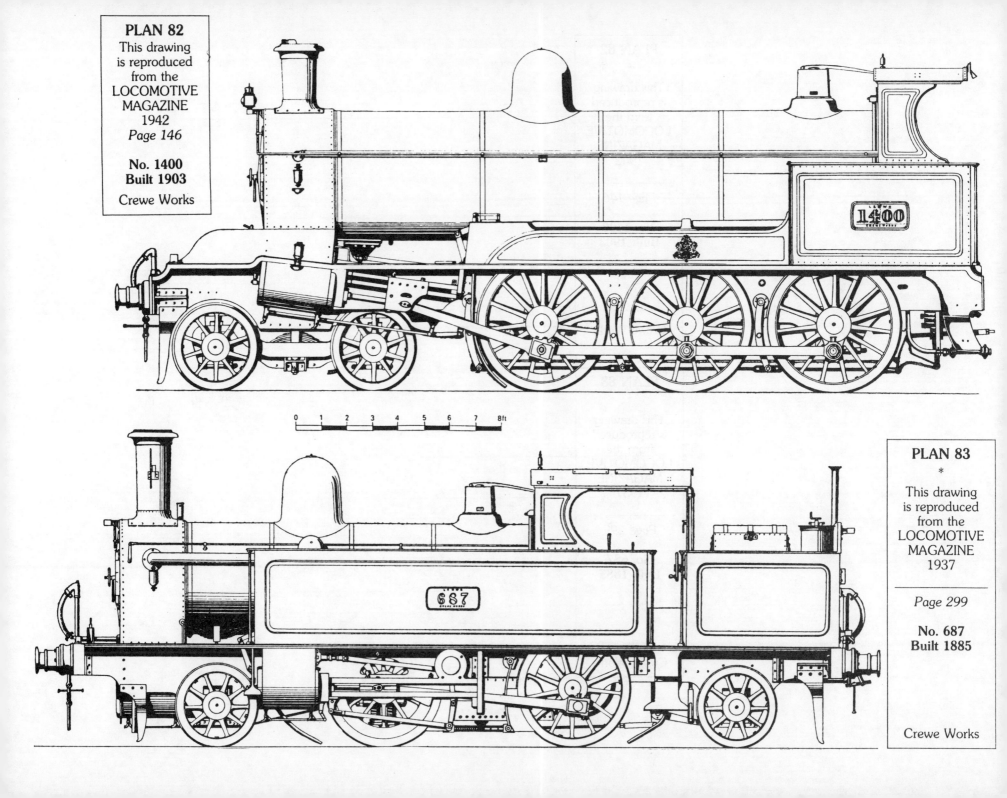

PLAN 82
This drawing
is reproduced
from the
LOCOMOTIVE
MAGAZINE
1942
Page 146

No. 1400
Built 1903

Crewe Works

1400

0 1 2 3 4 5 6 7 8ft

687

PLAN 83

*

This drawing
is reproduced
from the
LOCOMOTIVE
MAGAZINE
1937

Page 299

No. 687
Built 1885

Crewe Works

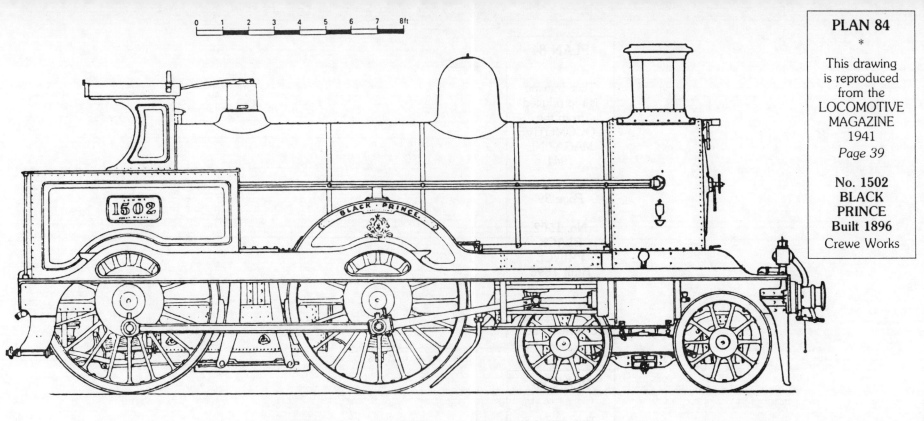

PLAN 84

*

This drawing
is reproduced
from the
LOCOMOTIVE
MAGAZINE
1941
Page 39

No. 1502
**BLACK
PRINCE**
Built 1896
Crewe Works

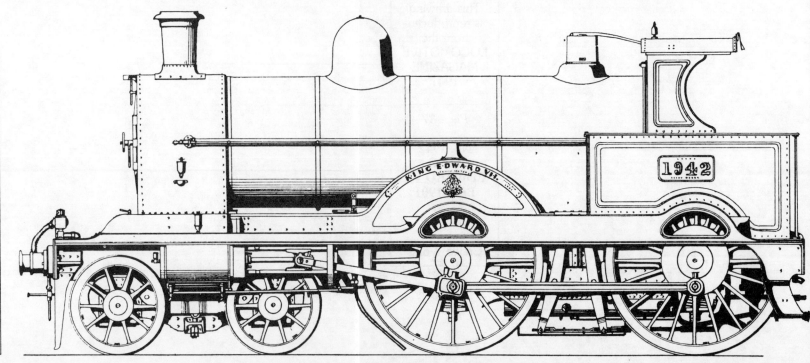

PLAN 85

*

This drawing
is reproduced
from the
LOCOMOTIVE
MAGAZINE
1941

Page 87

No. 1942
**KING
EDWARD VII**
Built 1901

Crewe Works

PLAN 84

*

This drawing
is reproduced
from the
LOCOMOTIVE
MAGAZINE
1941

Page 39

**No. 1502
BLACK
PRINCE
Built 1896**

Crewe Works

PLAN 85

*

This drawing
is reproduced
from the
LOCOMOTIVE
MAGAZINE
1941

Page 87

**No. 1942
KING
EDWARD VII
Built 1901**

Crewe Works

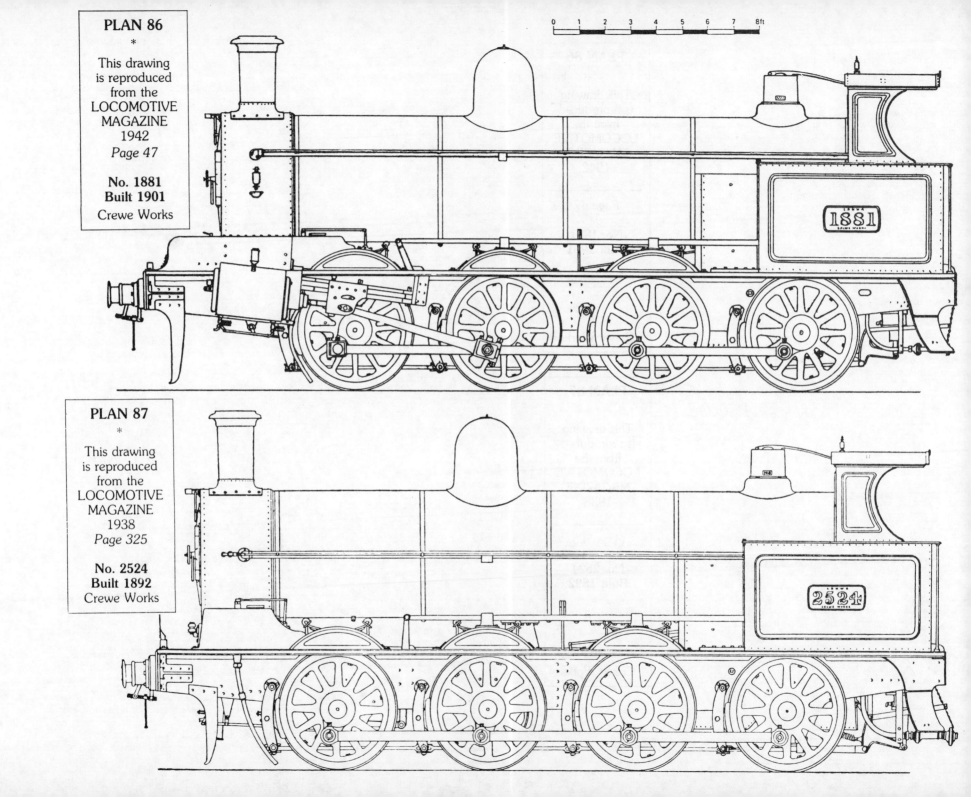

PLAN 86

*

This drawing
is reproduced
from the
LOCOMOTIVE
MAGAZINE
1942
Page 47

No. 1881
Built 1901
Crewe Works

0 1 2 3 4 5 6 7 8ft

1881

PLAN 87

*

This drawing
is reproduced
from the
LOCOMOTIVE
MAGAZINE
1938
Page 325

No. 2524
Built 1892
Crewe Works

2524

PLAN 86

*

This drawing
is reproduced
from the
LOCOMOTIVE
MAGAZINE
1942

Page 47

No. 1881
Built 1901

Crewe Works

PLAN 87

*

This drawing
is reproduced
from the
LOCOMOTIVE
MAGAZINE
1938

Page 325

No. 2524
Built 1892

Crewe Works

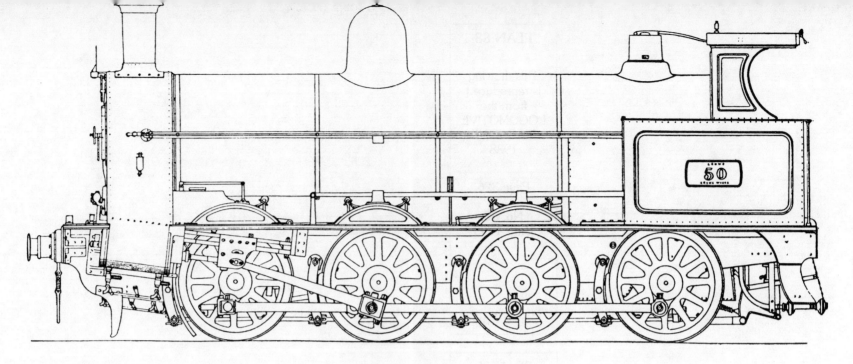

0 1 2 3 4 5 6 7 8ft

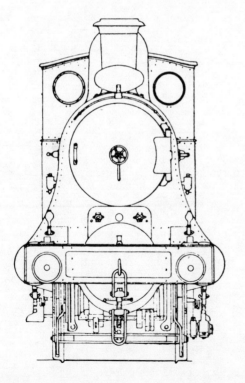

PLAN 88

*

This drawing
is reproduced
from the
LOCOMOTIVE
MAGAZINE
1938

Page 326

**No. 50
Built 1893**

Crewe Works

PLAN 89

*

This drawing
is reproduced
from the
LOCOMOTIVE
MAGAZINE
1938

**TINY
18″ GAUGE
LOCO
Built 1862**

Crewe Works

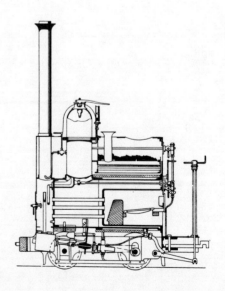

PLAN 88

*

This drawing
is reproduced
from the
LOCOMOTIVE
MAGAZINE
1938

Page 326

**No. 50
Built 1893**

Crewe Works

PLAN 89

*

This drawing
is reproduced
from the
LOCOMOTIVE
MAGAZINE
1938

**TINY
18″ GAUGE
LOCO
Built 1862**

Crewe Works

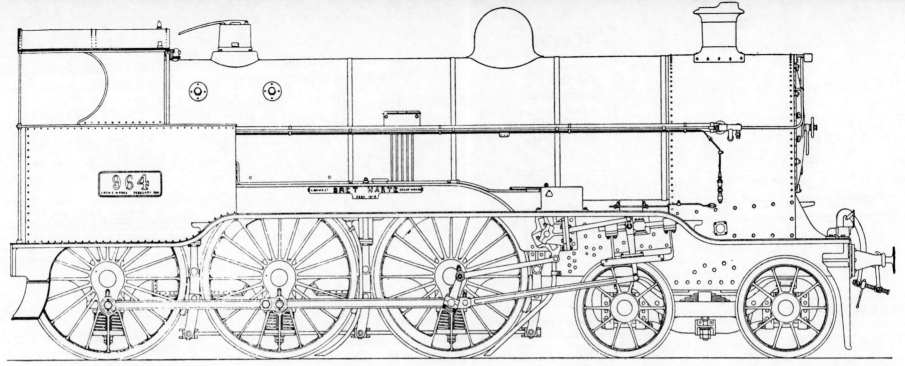

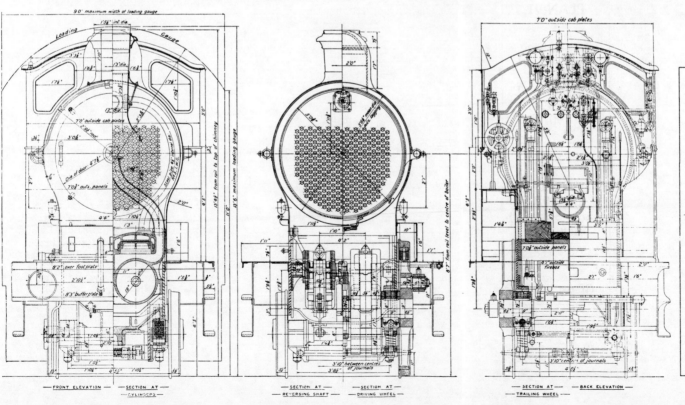

PLAN 91

*

This drawing
is reproduced
from the
LOCOMOTIVE
MAGAZINE
1907

Page 81

**MIXED
TRAFFIC
(Cross Sections)
Built 1907**

Crewe Works

PLAN 90

*

This drawing
is reproduced
from the
LOCOMOTIVE
MAGAZINE
1923

Page 158

**No. 964
BRET HARTE
Rebuilt 1922**

Crewe Works

— FRONT ELEVATION —   — SECTION AT —
CYLINDERS

— SECTION AT —   — SECTION AT —
REVERSING SHAFT   DRIVING WHEEL

— SECTION AT —   — BACK ELEVATION —
TRAILING WHEEL

PLAN 90

*

This drawing
is reproduced
from the
LOCOMOTIVE
MAGAZINE
1923

Page 158

**No. 964
BRET HARTE
Rebuilt 1922**

Crewe Works

PLAN 91

*

This drawing
is reproduced
from the
LOCOMOTIVE
MAGAZINE
1907

Page 81

**MIXED
TRAFFIC
(Cross Sections)
Built 1907**

Crewe Works

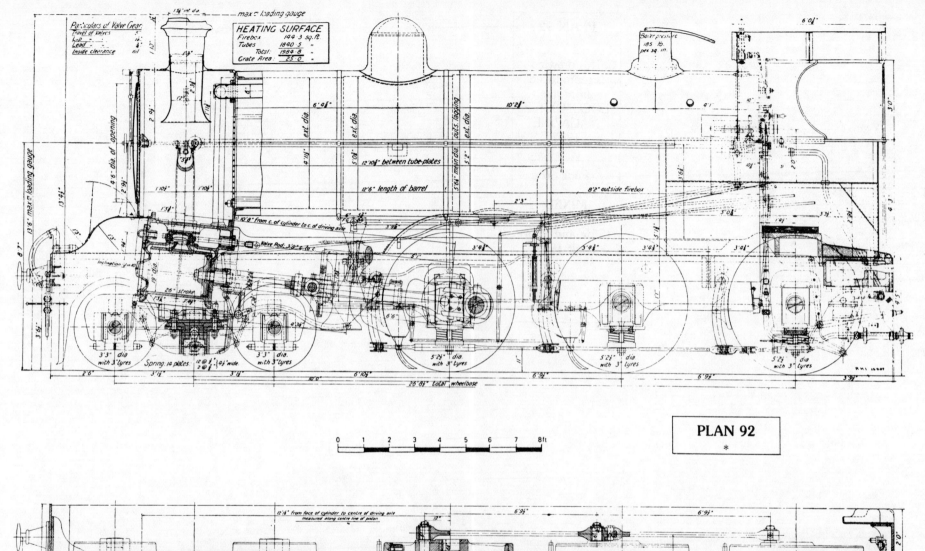

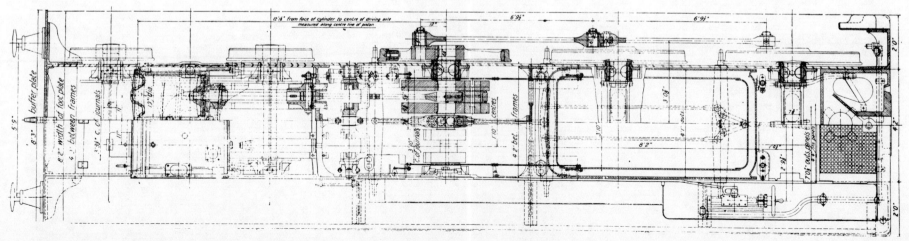

PLAN 92

*

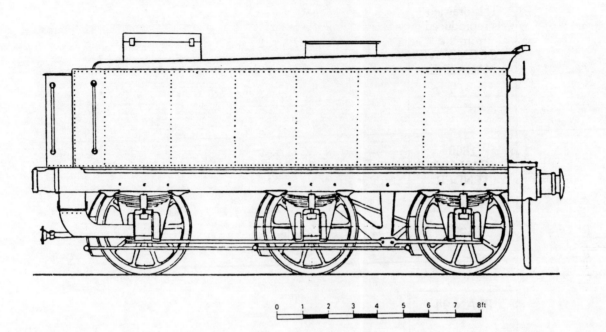

0   1   2   3   4   5   6   7   8ft

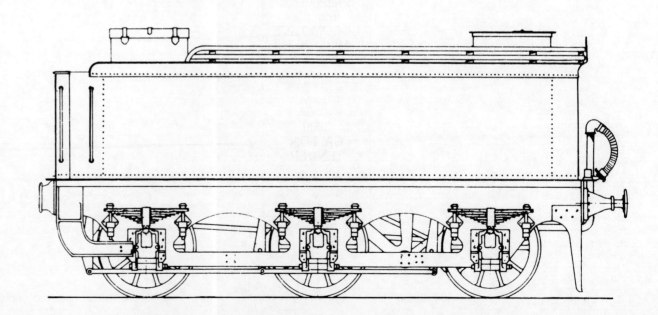

PLAN 93

*

This drawing
is reproduced
from the
LOCOMOTIVE
MAGAZINE

**1800
GALLON
TENDER**

PLAN 94

*

This drawing
is reproduced
from the
LOCOMOTIVE
MAGAZINE

**3000
GALLON
TENDER**

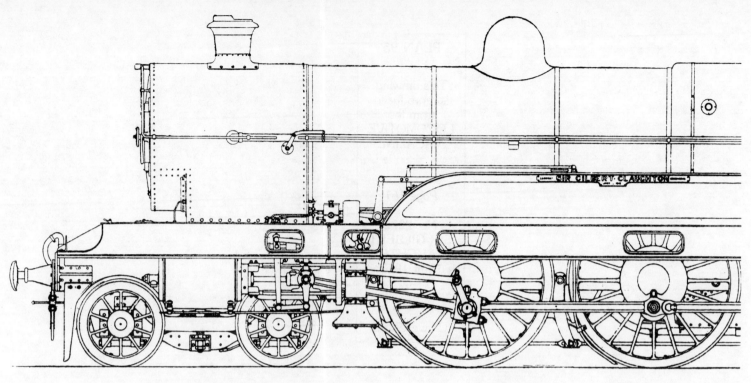

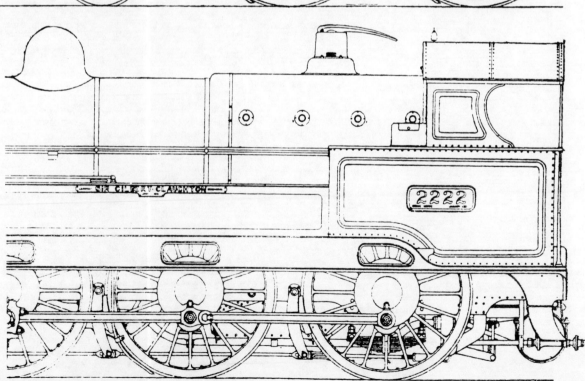

PLAN 95

*

This drawing
is reproduced
from the
LOCOMOTIVE
MAGAZINE

Page 161

No. 2222
SIR GILBERT
CLAUGHTON
Built 1913

Crewe Works